Endless October

by

Randy Schultz

This book is dedicated

To my lovely wife, BJ.

She loves me and, more important, my dogs.

For years, she has

encouraged me to write about my adventures.

I finally did it.

"Lord, please help me be the man my bird dog thinks I am."

Table of Contents

Montana
(Photo by Gary Thompson)

Foreword

I remember the awe I felt when I first saw a bird dog at work. I was in my late thirties, full of flying, family, and lifestyle. I knew there were such animals, and I remembered watching one work a field and point single birds, just using his nose.

I really liked the way they would freeze in place and not

move until the hunter walked in front of the dog and the bird flushed. I was so impressed the dog would be single-minded, methodical, and relentless in its search for the bird.

At the time, even though it was an exciting thing to watch, I couldn't see how I would ever be able to have a bird dog or train one to hunt. But, I stored all that in the back of my brain. Who could imagine the impact bird dogs would have on my life down the road?

A few years later, my friend and I would walk to our deer stands in the early morning. It was dark and cold, and we'd spent the night in anticipation of seeing the big buck. Vaguely, I knew, in the back of my head, sitting in a tree and waiting for a deer to walk by wasn't going to fulfill my urge to walk the country, see things, and work with animals. One dark morning, walking to the stands, I stepped into a covey of Bobwhite Quail. I yelled and looked around, still not understanding what happened. My friend laughed and said, "Quail won't hurt you!"

Ten yards further on, he stepped into a covey. His shout could be heard for miles. Once our heartbeats returned to near normal, we laughed and continued on to our stands. Every step, however, was in anticipation of another roar of wings in the night.

Long, boring hours in a deer stand lends to contemplation. I thought, "Maybe, I should get a bird dog. Apparently, we have quail on the lease. It might be a pleasant distraction. We have always been dog people."

The next day, I discussed it with my wife. Shortly after that, she presented me with a little, male Brittany puppy. The die was cast. I would forever be a bird dog man.

From that little Brittany, Rocket, through English Setters and more Brittanys, I learned what it meant to hunt birds with a dog. Every hunt would show me new things about dogs, and birds, and habitat.

I passed through all the many phases of the bird hunter's evolution, from relishing the kill, and counting coveys and single birds, through competing with other bird hunters, looking for the "best" dog, and making the perfect point, shot, and retrieve combination. Finally, the end result is what others would call "The Zen of Bird Hunting." Taking time to sit and look at the prairie, forest, swamp, desert, wheat field, or corn stubble and marvel, at the dog and the team, and at God's Creation and what a small, little piece of that puzzle we are.

By then, the journey was the destination. The way the dogs handled birds, the complete cycle of finding the bird, pointing, shooting, and retrieving the bird, all done perfectly, became much more important than numbers of birds in the bag. Traveling to different states to hunt different species of upland birds with different dogs became important to me.

I retired from flying at a major airline, and, suddenly, I became free to pursue my passion.

These stories are not chronological, nor are they ordered by topic. They are the result of years of learning, observing, and making mistakes. Most are included in my blog, which you can find at www.abirdhuntersthoughts.com.

All of them are from the heart. One story, about the passing of my dog, Ace, is still (years later) too difficult for me to read, even though I wrote it. I do encourage you to read it, though. I even have a story of a moose encounter while growing up in Alaska, which includes no dogs, at all, but illustrates, a little bit, how I came to love the outdoors.

October is the finest month in the calendar for a bird hunter. Many states open their seasons on five different species of grouse, pheasant, and Hungarian Partridge in October. It's the time of fall colors, crisp mornings, and warm afternoons. It comes in gently, and leaves with a blizzard. October is never far from my thoughts-no matter what the calendar shows. In fact, in the remaining years God grants me to be here, I hope to be living an endless October.

Cap and His First Sharptail Grouse

1. Bird Bag Memories

It was the end of the season, and time to clean guns and gear. My bird vest was piled in the back of the truck. I looked in the bird bag at the sticks, feathers, wool hats, spent shells, an empty plastic bottle, and various other items, and started thinking about the contents.

There were some Sharptail Grouse feathers from my September trip to Montana. I recalled Ruby (B/F/1.5yrs) loping along the sagebrush hills and spinning to point a plum thicket absolutely full of Sharptails. Ace (B/M/7yrs) working the edge of a green alfalfa field, dropping into the creek for a quick dip, climbing out up the steep bank and slamming a point on a small covey of Sharps on a forty-five-degree slope.

And Cap (B/M/1.5yrs) disappearing around a clay mound, one hot day, forcing me to walk around the hill looking for him, only to find him standing tall on a covey of seven or eight Sharps.

A few small Hungarian Partridge feathers were mixed in the brew, I think from the day Ace and I managed to corner six coveys just before sunset with the temperature dropping and a long walk back to the truck.

One long rooster tail feather fell out on the floor. Possibly this feather was from the bad boy rooster Cap and I worked alongside the gravel road outside Regent, N.D. Cap worked him, pointed, worked him, pointed – for almost 200 yards. He was careful not to push too hard, and it was a pleasure to watch him, a pup, just a year-and-a-half old, work the bird like a much older, seasoned dog.

Finally, the rooster made a fatal mistake and veered to the road and the edge of the CRP grass. He stopped and, following right on his scent, Cap locked up, high and tight. For some reason, I just knew this was a rooster and a big one at that. Sure enough, he got up, squawking and flapping, right over Cap's head, banked right, and headed for Canada. A load of 5's caught him square and the puppy made a great retrieve to hand. A little bird dog love fest ensued for a few minutes, right there on the prairie, as we celebrated Cap's first Rooster.

Mixed with the feathers, a wool watch cap came out. Nancy, I have your hat. Remember when we hunted along CJ Strike Reservoir in Idaho? It was cold that morning, but warmed up nicely. You aren't but five foot nothing and hauling all that camera gear, I guess, will warm you up. I don't remember the hat going into my bird bag, but I know it's yours. I'll return it the next time I'm in Idaho.

Valley Quail feathers from the sloughs and plum thickets in Idaho were in the mix. Probably from the day we had 40+ points in an area maybe a half mile on a side. Four dogs either backing or pointing a small shrub with fifteen quail hunkered down inside. We took pictures and took our time and finally kicked the bush and shot a bird or two. What a fun that day was ... cold and damp and perfect.

My favorite feathers of the trip I hold to the last – my Chukar feathers from Idaho. Cap on point, Aaron, my friend, and his dog, Remy, working up alongside and the birds getting up over the volcanic rocks and heading down into the steep canyon. I knocked one down and Cap gave chase. He made a retrieve that still brings a grin to my face and the little Brit put that Chukar in my hand. He looked up and said, "Hey, Boss, there's more in here! Let's get 'em!"

An old plastic water bottle from Minnesota with a Ruffed Grouse feather still stuck to the side brought memories of Ace panting and staring and as immobile as a marble statue, alongside the trail as I came around the bend. The light roar of wings as the male Ruff headed to cover, just a split second too late. Ace put the bird in my hand with a slight wink as we acknowledged each other's contribution to the evening meal.

Not a bad year for memories, I think, as I clean out the spent shells (#5's, #6's, and #7½'s), twigs, collapsible water bowls and one lone penny. I tossed the penny back in. I hope next season will fill the bird bag just as full. If not with birds, then I'll be happy and content with the memories of good bird dogs, fine companionship, bright blue skies and birds rising over the pointed dog, while the twin barrels come up and safety clicks off.

Cap and Randy

2. Dog Bragging and Chickens

I was hunting in the great state of Michigan, chasing the King of Gamebirds, the Ruffed Grouse. The habitat was perfect. The day was a little warm, in the 60s; the sky was overcast and we had a little breeze. It was, all in all, a perfect day to be in the grouse woods.

As I unloaded dogs and proceeded with the goat-rope involving excited bird dogs, tracking collars, vests, water, guns, and trucks, I noticed an older man with worn boots, scarred leather gloves, battered hat, and patched trousers walking down the two-track road.

He was toting an old double in one hand, and his other hand gripped a lead attached to a very high-energy, liver Brittany.

Seeing as bird hunters generally are a small group and Ruff hunters are an even smaller group, I took the time to corral my dogs and greet the old man. We made some small talk about the birds, cover, weather, and even old shotguns.

Finally, the conversation turned to bird dogs. Since he was a man of discernment, as I could plainly see the beautiful male Brit at the end of the tether, I asked if he thought the pup was going to be a great dog. He smiled ruefully and said, "In my youth, I would brag on my dogs like they were part of the Second Coming! Now, I keep my mouth shut. I've found the moment I bragged on any dog, the die was cast and I was in for a real adventure with him. Let me tell you about one morning, right here in these Michigan woods ..."

The old man turned out that fateful morning with his two males on the ground. It was a good combination of dogs – the 6-year-old superstar, and a 3-year-old up-and-comer. He knew these woods held grouse, and he was ready for an enjoyable morning. The 6-year-old was his best dog, and everyone who knew him, knew his dog.

He wasn't shy about bragging on the liver Brit (some might say it approached obnoxious, but any bird dog man would say that's impossible!).

So, off they went down the trail, the old man with a 20 ga. double in hand. After a half-mile or so, he noticed the young dog was still working well, crossing the trail and working either side, but the other boy hadn't checked in for a while. A glance at the GPS told him he was .21 miles out. Not concerned, he toned him and expected him to turn back and check in, as he worked with the younger dog getting him in to some great cover.

A short time later, he glanced at the GPS again, and saw the other dog (let's just call the wonder-dog "Cap" for the sake of clarity) was now .42 miles out! Slightly alarmed, the old man blew his whistle and switched his GPS to map mode to see where the boy was headed.

Relieved, he saw only a creek and an old dirt road in front of the moving triangle, .75 miles out now. He raised his double and fired twice, and blew his whistle again, while watching the map. Cap stopped, circled, and headed out once more! At 1.2 miles out, Cap hit the dirt road and started back to the truck.

Whew, thought the old guy, he's come to his senses and will be joining the party in a little bit. Then, Cap reversed course and headed away, down the dirt road. He was now 1.5 miles out and running down the road.

The man yelled to his other pup, reversed course and moved as fast as his old legs could carry him back to the truck. He crated the young dog, removed his vest, stowed his gun, and closed the tailgate – all in record time.

He cranked the diesel and turned around on the two-track, throwing leaves and dirt as he accelerated toward the dirt road his dog was running. Then, 1.75 miles out and approaching some private parcels along the road, Cap's little marker seemed to stop and then move in circles. The old man turned a corner just in time to see his prized, champion, perfect bird dog holding on to a big yard chicken by the tail feathers!

He slammed to a stop and glanced at the house and noticed the big picture window facing the alleged altercation. At this point, the feathers came out of the chicken and she made some very tight right and left turns – all to no avail, as the highly trained BIRD dog pounced on her. Cap looked up, saw the truck and the agitated old man running to him, and made a perfect retrieve to hand.

"Where in the world have you been?" Cap said. "Here, I've got something for you!"

The man took the chicken as Cap jumped into the front seat of the truck, covering the seat in feathers, mud and slime. As the man climbed the steps of the house, he could only worry about how much this now-expired chicken was going to cost him.

Since that episode, the old man explained, he's refrained from bragging on any dog, because, at any given moment, any dog can lose his mind and act like a complete fool.

Round Two

The very next year, passing through Michigan, I had a little time to kill. I decided to attempt contact with the owners of the deceased chicken and explain what happened.

It was the Day of Reckoning. It was time to 'fess up and do the right thing, albeit somewhat late.

I drove to the area, found the house, and knocked on the door again. No one was home. I was a little relieved, but in an effort to get this behind me, I drove down the dirt road looking for anyone I could find. Two houses down, a man was sitting on his porch. As I pulled up to his house, I was wondering just how I was going to explain this. I introduced myself and we made some small talk about the weather, hunting Ruffs, bird dogs, etc.

Finally, I just came out with it, and explained the situation. I told him about Cap (who was peering out the passenger side window – undoubtedly scanning for chickens), about hunting in the area, chasing the dog down, finding him in the neighbor's yard with a chicken in his mouth. He was chuckling the whole time. I told him I was glad someone found it funny, but would he mind telling the neighbor (who was a mailman and never home during the day) I came back to face the music and explain the situation. By this time, his chuckling had turned to outright laughter. I offered to pay whatever the going rate was for yard chickens, if he would pass it along to his neighbor.

With tears rolling down his face, he said I could keep my money. It was worth it, having provided entertainment for the past year among the four or five houses clustered along the river. He told me the story of the neighbor finding the dead chicken on the door stoop and asking around as to the means of its demise. No one would confess, so it was generally agreed the local Black Lab (who wandered in from across the road) was the culprit. Poor old Bob was in hot water for a week or so, he said. But, life got back to normal, and the "dead chicken incident" passed into the lore of the community.

I was relieved there were no problems among the neighbors due to me and my bird dog. We talked a while longer (he was a Navy vet, as well) and it was time for me and my chicken-killing Brittany to move along. I told him thanks and headed for my truck.

"Wait a minute," he yelled,"you should apologize to Old Bob before you leave!" So, I did. I walked to the dog, curled up under a pine tree, gave him a treat, and told him I was sorry for framing him for the killing of the chicken – and Cap was sorry, too. Old Bob just devoured the treat and rolled over for a tummy rub. I guess that was about as forgiven as I was going to get. I was happy to get it. All in all, we can learn a lot from dogs.

BJ and Cap in North Dakota

3. The $200 Shotgun

It seems that some time in the distant past, I might, or might not, have mentioned to my wife, that, although I do have several shotguns, they are all inexpensive. In fact, the story goes, she says I told her none of my guns cost more than $200.

While neither confirming nor denying said statement was made, I do admit I was guilty for allowing the misunderstanding to exist. Over the years, as shotguns were acquired, I assured my lovely bride that I would never pay more for them than the usual amount.

And, so, life blissfully carried on, until that fateful day, in my barn, during a field trial. It was cold and raining so several of my bird dog friends were warming themselves by the fire and talking about all things bird hunting. BJ, my bride, joined us for a bit. She usually holds her own in these meetings regaling the audience with stories of my (mis)adventures with various dogs. Laughter and good-natured ribbing was the name of the game, and everyone chipped in to tell an anecdote about their favorite dog or hunt.

Conversation got around to shotguns and who just bought what, the various makes and models and quality thereof. Finally, someone happened to spy the gun I'd set aside as I came in from my brace and asked if that was the old A. H. Fox, and why would I use it in such bad weather. I explained I liked to shoot the gun, and I would probably spend quite a while cleaning and oiling after the day was over.

Another friend opined that he would never allow a gun like that to get wet, and so on. I happened to glance at my wife and noticed a puzzled look on her face. Warning flags shot up ("Danger, Will Robinson! Danger!"). But then, BJ smiled and announced that it was no big deal, since "None of Randy's shotguns cost more than $200 anyway." (At this point in the tale, you could hear the wind blowing dust in the empty street and the hawk screech high overhead.)

Mouths opened, jaws dropped and men froze in place. After a long, quiet moment, "Absolutely!" "Yes!" "Uh huh!" "Yep, that's right, BJ!" was heard throughout the barn.

Then, slowly, the laughter started and I heard several of my "friends" offering to BJ the supposed value of a few of my $200 guns. It was generally acknowledged, among the crowd, that I was dog meat for the rest of the year. I would never see the Dakotas, Montana, Minnesota, Kansas, Texas, Wisconsin, or New Mexico again (or, at least, during my natural lifetime).

She laughed and enjoyed my discomfort for a while, and then gave me big kiss, bowed out, and headed back to the house. She laughed again and said she needed to get moving. "It's a long drive to Atlanta, honey, and you don't mind if I do a little shopping, do you? Oh, and I promise not to get anything that costs more than $200! Honest!"

There's a lesson there ... somewhere.

Randy and Bo
(Photo by Tammy Jarrett)

4. The Bullfight

Bo made his mark field trialing, but he was first, foremost, and always, a "wild bird" dog. Intense, determined, smart, and driven to find birds, he could be a handful at times. Just keeping track of him was problematic some days. I would see him get birdy and follow scent for half a mile before finally locking down – "Here they are, boss!"

Normally, I would teach my dogs to keep me in sight and hunt for me. Bo pretty much considered that backwards – I was there to shoot for him.

But first, I had to find him to do my job. It gave the term "hunting dog" new meaning. That's what I was doing some days- just hunting for my dog. He could disappear off a trail in Wisconsin in the blink of an eye. I would be sure he was just around the corner, and I would hear his beeper soon. Thirty agonizing minutes later, I'd hear the faintest sound of his beeper – either on point or returning through the forest. Usually, he'd show up, admonish me for getting lost, and warn me to keep up.

The grouse woods were the worst. Thick and vast, a dog that liked to "get out there" would disappear fast. Every year, I would see posters for lost dogs at the local vet and in the entrance at local cafes and bars. I also heard of many happy endings, but, many times, only a collar and fur would be found. The grouse woods are no place for an untrained dog.

Bo, on the other hand, was far from untrained. To his mind, scent meant birds, and when he hit scent it was time to find the birds – no matter where or how far. Bo's bullfight didn't occur in the woods of Wisconsin or Minnesota, but in the rolling hills of

Nebraska – a place I thought, for sure, I'd be able to keep him in sight.

We put out on public land. It was nine in the morning and the day was cold and clear, and the sky was crystal blue with a heavy frost on the ground. This was day one of a two-week odyssey. Since he had seniority, I slipped Bo out of his kennel and notched the beeper around his neck. We had a little talk about staying in sight and he jumped off the tailgate to find some birds.

We started down a brushy draw looking for some local pheasant. I'd heard some cackling that morning and knew some birds were in the vicinity. I watched the bonehead work brush along the cornfields, along a tree claim, and over a small rise.

Suddenly, his beeper went off and I hustled over the hill to find him locked down tight in some tall grass by a small stand of thick brush. The gun was loaded for pheasant when a huge covey of quail blew out of there! I dropped one, but the 4's I had in there for pheasant pretty much made a mess of the poor thing.

It was shaping up to be fine day, though. Bo made a good retrieve to hand and we gathered our wits and headed out again. "Good job, old boy!" I thought as I watched that setter tail go over the next rise. And that was the last time I saw him.

As I crested the rise, I saw that the obvious route for him

would be down to a small creek bed. It turned in to a ditch, then gully, and finally a pretty deep gorge. I called and whistled and listened for his beeper – nothing.

I waited about an hour in the general area. Finally, I headed back to the truck to get another dog. I covered the area several times and worked a mile in every direction throughout the day. No dog, no tracks. Nothing. I wasn't panicked at that point – I'd seen this act before.

We headed for the truck and started driving the roads in the likely direction of travel. I talked to farmers and other hunters. We swapped cell numbers and war stories about lost dogs and they promised to look out for Bo.

I got stuck in the mud pretty bad one time and spent hours working to get back on the gravel road. Finally, a tractor as big as a barn showed up and pulled me on to the dry land. It seems he watched me for a while from his barn, until he couldn't stand it any more. He had to come down and help the flatlander get moving again! (This was only one of the many times I've depended on the largesse of a farmer with a huge tractor.)

By now, it was getting late. The last time I saw Bo, it was 9:45 in the morning. It was now 5:45 p.m. and getting dark fast.

The temperature was dropping and the wind was picking up, and I was beginning to go from concerned to really worried.

The nights up there can be really bad, especially for a shaggy eared mutt from Georgia with no place to get warm.

I drove the roads in the area one more time, hoping to see tracks crossing. I stopped every hundred yards and blew the whistle and listened for the beeper. Nothing. Finally, I turned the truck toward the nearest small town and slowly headed for a local motel.

I crested a rise and my cell phone rang. My poor wife yelled "Hey, they found Bo!"

"Where?" I yelled back.

"I don't know, but here's the guy's number."

I pulled to the side of the road, wrote it down and called the number. Sure enough, the young man who answered had Bo. He gave me directions to his place – seven miles away!

We kicked the diesel into gear and made good time to the barn and my wayward dog. When we pulled up, the knothead was on the back of a young man's truck drinking water from a jug. I thanked him profusely while checking Bo over for cuts, scratches or wounds. He was in good shape, so I loaded him in to his dog box and went back to talk to the farmer and thank him again.

The young man explained that he only checks his cows a few times during the week and Bo was lucky today was one of those days. When he drove up to the barn, there was a ruckus going on inside. He opened the door and saw a bunch of dust flying around the bull's pen. His huge bull had a dog cornered in the pen and was about one minute away from smashing that white setter into the dirt.

The farmer grabbed a shock stick, backed the bull off, grabbed the dog by the collar and pulled him out of there. It was a near thing, he explained. His bull is a mean, nasty boy when he's around his cows. It was fortunate he was able to get there in time. Once more, I thanked him for his consideration and we drove out of there. And, once again, I was thankful for the generosity of the American farmer.

As Bo and I chatted about the event, he related how I got lost and he went looking for me for a few hours. Finally, he got so thirsty; he went down in to the creek bed. It was frozen, so he followed it for a bit until he came upon the stock tanks. He was in the inside tank working on his third lap when some rude, cranky, mean old slab of hamburger took offense at his joining the party.

Bo allowed as how he was willing to let all this mean-spirited talk go and be on his way, but a few choice words were tossed about, and Bo said he might or might not have made a few comments as to what the bull's momma may or may not have done.

Well, that was that- the fight was on. Bo told me he was giving as good he got – the bull was mean and big, but Bo was fast, smart, and wiry. In fact, Bo was a little miffed at the farmer because, as he tells it: "I had that stupid piece of hamburger right where I wanted him, Boss – overconfident and right in front of me! I was in the process of telling him I was going to whip his ample butt six ways from midnight and then go service all his cows, when the farmer came in and rescued him! If you ask me, it was that bull's lucky day."

Well, now I had a small problem. Who was I going to believe; my best bird dog or the eyes of the farmer? The choice was obvious. It was that bull's lucky day.

Bo with pheasant in the Noll ditch

5. The Noll Ditch

Hunting the Dakotas is always a special treat. I find the states to be dog and hunter friendly with few hazards for the dogs. (The main problems are skunks, porcupines, and the occasional strand of barbed wire.)

South Dakota is well known for its pheasant hunting, the result of a wonderful PR department and lots of dollars in advertising. It's great the state is using another crop (pheasant) to bring dollars into the local economy.

Less well known is North Dakota. I've hunted both states

and prefer the northern one for ease of hunting and, to my subjective impression, just as many (or more) birds. It may take a trip or two to find a location that suits you, but the rewards are many. The folks are friendly, the birds plentiful and the country is breath-taking in its horizon-to-horizon wheat and corn field beauty.

One October, many years ago. I was hunting with my English Setter, Bo, and my Brittany, Rocket. My hunting companions were off exploring for new areas, and I had the day off to enjoy my dogs and the country by myself. I figured I'd go see a friend who lived about an hour away. I've hunted Gerry's ditch through his cornfield for so many years that we watched his boy, Danny, grow up, get married and have kids.

This adventure started a lot of years ago on a hot, dry October day. We were driving the back roads looking for a likely place to put out and bust up a few pheasant. We noticed a perfect spot, a wide ditch about a mile long with a stream in the center between two cornfields. Perfect. And right across the road, two fellows were up on an old house repairing the roof. We pulled in to ask permission to hunt. I shouted up to them. They didn't say anything. Then, the bigger guy started coming down the ladder. Like most North Dakota farmers, he didn't make a lot of small talk. "Yeah, you can hunt it. But after you're done, we will be in that building over there and you'd better show up to tell us how it went! Hey, did you guys drive all the way from Georgia just to hunt these ditch-chickens? (Yep.) Anybody that crazy deserves a chance at the creek- that's for sure!"

Gerry turned back around and headed up that ladder. "You'd better show up, Georgia-boy," he yelled over his shoulder.

We hunted, had a great time, and we showed up to tell him all about it. A friendship developed over the years and we always made it a point to hunt that ditch, even in bad years. It's not about hunting the ditch for pheasant any more.

So, Bo, Rocket, and I headed over to hunt the ditch and catch up on what was happening in the county over the last year. We rolled in to the farm, but it was empty – harvesting probably– so we drove across the road to the round bales piled up along the creek and parked. I let Bo out all by himself – just the knothead and me this time.

He ducked the barbed wire and flew down to the little creek, tail snapping and nose to the ground as I straddled the wire and worked my way over the fence. By the time I made it across, loaded my gun and found the whistle, I heard the "beep, beep, beep" of Bo's collar on point. He was only 20 yards away locked down tight on a clump of sage, near some weeds, and under a few scraggly trees in a bend in the creek. His signature stance – low, head stretched out, tail up to about the 10 o'clock position, and per-fectly still – was a thing of beauty to me.

As I moved to him, I checked the old A.H. Fox 20 ga. was loaded and safe, my hat was down to shade my eyes from the sun, and I was alone with no people, cows, or other dogs around.

I moved around a little to the side to get a better shooting lane and to keep from walking directly up from behind him, letting him know where I was. As I got within 10 yards, the bush exploded with feathers, squawking, and beating wings! Two big old rooster pheasant boiled out of that bush and headed airborne to the corn field.

It's amazing what the mind can do – I remember the color of their red and white heads, the blue of the sky, the white of Bo's tail, the light brown of the sandy grass, the smell of the sage and the gurgle of the creek! The Fox fit my shoulder perfectly as I dropped the bird on the right – dead!

Bo was on it immediately. He picked up the big bird and trotted over to put it in my hand. "Here, Boss, nice shooting!"he would say, and we would be off again. (The thousand times that event took place over the years never seemed to change, yet every time was fresh and exciting, dog and man harvesting game.)

A little farther down, we managed to trap another pheasant, up against the creek in some tall grass. A short time later, I heard Bo's beeper again. As I scanned down the creek, looking for his white tail, I saw him stretched out at the top of the draw coming down out of the corn field. He had a big rooster pinned only feet from the top. The cagey, old bird had an escape route all mapped out, but Bo was too fast for him and caught him before he could make it to the corn.

I climbed the gray, clay wall up behind the dog hoping the bird would wait until I got into shooting distance. Finally, about 10 yards from the dog, a big rooster cackled and exploded from in front of Bo's nose. He almost made it to the corn.

It was a long and satisfying walk back to the truck. Three roosters in the game bag can be a load, but this was an easy carry. I called Bo in and we walked together across land we just hunted, chatting about the day and the flushes and the wily ones that got away.

I made it to the barn just as Gerry and Danny were getting in from cutting corn, and I lived it all over again as I told them about one of the best days I'd had in North Dakota. Not many men are as lucky to be able to hunt where and when they want.

And no one is as lucky as I am to have a long-tailed, shaggy-eared, spotted, school-flunking, curly-tailed setter to hunt over, either. The adventures of "The Bocephus" bring a smile to my lips every time; even as I mutter, "That scrawny, knothead's done it again ...!"

Wisconsin grouse woods

6. Grouse Woods Buffoonery

The day was promising. It was 25 degrees, clear with light wind. I scouted the area the day before and knew the trail and likely habitat I would find, even though I was a newbie to this part of the National Forest.

My main dog, Ace, was itching to go but that was not necessarily a good thing. Ace is a male Brittany, a big running, fast, smart, bold, confident Brittany. I knew there was a good chance he would take to the woods as he had done in the North Dakota plains we'd left just two days before.

Out on the prairie, I would turn him out, turn on the GPS, and wait for the pager to go off. When it did, Ace would be on point, with some pheasant pinned down in the CRP grass, awaiting my arrival with the shotgun.

It had worked hundreds of times during the six-and-a-half years we hunted together. The rooster might run, but he was usually close when I got there. The flush, shot, and loading the big bird in the game bag was routine.

The grouse woods require a much more patient dog, just as smart, but slower working, cautious ... a thinker. Good grouse dogs are a rarity and a treasure to be hoarded and protected. Boldness, while an asset in hunting quail, Pheasant, Sharptail Grouse, and Hungarian Partridge, is a detriment while hunting Ruffed Grouse.

So, I had a talk with the boy and it was like telling the quarterback to not kiss the Prom Queen – he rolled his eyes as if to say, "Pops, I know what I'm doing here! Just unhook the lead and I'll show you some grouse hunting!"

With not a little trepidation, I let him go, loaded my gun, marked the truck, took a compass heading, looked up ... and he was gone!

Before I had time to walk 100 yards up the trail, I looked at the GPS and that knothead was 650 yards into the woods ... and accelerating!

I just kept walking the trail and occasionally pulled the GPS in map mode to watch his track. Before long, he swung around and came loping up the trail with a grin (a little lipstick on his collar) and an attitude to match. I grabbed him, "counselled" him once more, and turned him loose.

Another 400+ yard. cast. Frustration!

Finally, he decided hunting with me made more sense, and we continued the hunt for the illusive Ruffed Grouse with a now functional man-dog team. And we were rewarded with a very good day in the woods.

We stuck to the Aspen thickets and edges of clearings. Ace pointed several birds that were shootable and I did my thing over my dog.

I sprayed lead at several birds, and was occasionally rewarded with the "thump" of a bird hitting the forest floor

As often happens, the most memorable times come when you least expect them. Ace locked up in some very thick Aspens. He was only 40 yards away, and I was on him quickly. As grouse often do, this boy waited until I was behind a shrub and flushed over my head, out of a tree. I twisted and shot, missed, and watched him jink his way through the tree trunks.

I immediately headed after him (ignoring the smirk from my canine) telling Ace, "Easy, boy! Bird in here!"

We reached the area I saw him go down, and Ace started a circular search – he was birdy and a little frustrated and not getting the full scent. I relaxed a little and looked back to the spot of the initial flush and double checked my location. I was in the correct spot. So, I watched Ace work it out and pondered birds and flushes and bird hunting and Prom Queens. For no particular reason, I looked up and saw Mr. Grouse sitting on an Aspen limb not 20 feet away! I took a step and stomped and yelled, and he launched himself off the branch ... directly at my head!

I ducked and turned and shot twice at the retreating gray blur, missing twice. I twisted so fast and hard I overshot and had to look back over my shoulder to get his heading. I literally screwed myself into the ground.

This time, I called to Ace and started out on the heading of the retreating grouse, into a stand of planted pines that were perhaps 60 feet tall. Once again, I reached the area and let Ace do his thing. Once again, he was frustrated.

I stood and listened to the breeze in the pines, and the quiet ... and, way back of my consciousness, I heard a little flurry, just the faintest of sounds, almost unrecognizable. I looked up and down, unfocused my eyes and scanned the trees for movement, or sound, or anything.

I saw nothing but the pines and felt breeze and soft needles underfoot. Just then I noticed the tiniest little feather floating down, not three feet from my nose. I checked the light wind and realized that scoundrel had been in the tree right in front of me, perhaps ten feet over my head. That sound I almost heard was him launching off to safety.

I laughed and tipped my hat to the old boy. I hope he lived

long and sired many more just like him. Surely, he was a worthy opponent.

Ace
(Photo by Gary Thompson)

7. We Sat Together, Ace and I

The old dog and I put out on a day that was cool, as the sun was dropping. It was about an hour above the Montana horizon. This was a special spot. Last year, he and I moved 16 coveys of Huns and Sharptails in the Alfalfa fields, along the creek and below the hills that rose up out of the creek bottom.

He moved slower now, but still watched me and bounced around, and woofed at me to hurry up. All he needed was for me to take a step in the direction I wanted to go, and he would move out, nose up, quartering in the wind, searching for the scent of whatever game-bird this particular piece of country had to offer. Ten seasons, almost forty trips, tens of thousands of miles driven, added up to a wise old bird dog that had seen and done it all.

As a young dog, he was blazing fast. He never out-ran his nose, and he was all business. In NSTRA trials, he would make an initial cast and loop back around to me as I left the start line. Many was the time the judge would make the mistake of staying with me, instead of going after the brown blur off the line. After a minute, with him still gone, I would tell him, "You'd better go find him. If he's not back by now, he's on point."

Sure enough, I'd watch the judge head out and eventually raise his hand "Point!" the Judge would yell, and I'd hustle to get to my big Brittany.

Now, he wasn't so fast, but the heart was just as big, the desire to please me just as intense.

We left the truck, and the howling dogs still in their kennels, and I stepped into the knee-deep alfalfa, watching the old dog work the wind. It didn't take long before the head came up, the movement became precise and calculated to put that nose right in the middle of the scent cone. A few minor adjustments and he froze. The point lacked the quivering intensity of past years and, perhaps, some of the style, but the nose was deadly and the knowledge of how to treat these birds was still spot-on. A single bird got up, and the old boy watched it fall and put it in my hand.

A stroke on the side of the head, a drink of water, and a "Good boy!" and he was off again, quartering the wind, checking objectives and glancing at me (so quickly, it was hard to discern) to stay in front.

After a half-mile of this and another bird in the bag, I gave him a long wail on the whistle to call him in and we took a break and sat together on the top of a levee. We shared some water, and he allowed as to how I was shooting pretty good today. I accepted the praise gracefully, knowing he's seen quite the opposite many, many times.

I took off my beat-up hat and thanked God for this old dog and the time I was allowed to hunt with him. We are reminded, in the Book, that life is nothing more than a vapor in strong wind and is over in a flash. That wind blows so much stronger regarding the short lives of our hunting dogs. It seems a cruel joke on us, that we love our dogs so much and their lives are so short.

I struggle to my feet, using the old double gun like a crutch, as the dog takes off into the wind once more.

He slowed up considerably and limped constantly, now. But, he knew where he wanted to go to find the birds. It pained me to watch him with the swollen elbow and the lack of grace he had had in abundance as a younger dog.

Almost to the truck, at the end of the last field, he turned and locked up once again. Breathing hard, I could see he was tiring. The thought crossed my mind, this might be his last hunt. I quickly discarded that notion: "No. Surely he has a few years left in him!", and quickly walked to where he showed me the bird was hiding.

The big Sharpie got up and I unloaded both barrels at him, managing to hit him but not knock him down, he glided down through some trees and in to the field below as I lost sight of him.

Ace watched him, too, and glared back at me before trotting down the hill, through the trees and out in to the next field. I quickly followed, not willing to be chastised again by the old campaigner for not keeping up. His nose picked up the scent and he went straight to the bird. He brought it to me and, this time, he set it on the ground and dropped down next to it. It was the last bird he would retrieve.

He's fading fast now, three weeks later. We took him to the local University Vet School to see if there was anything to be done. The doctors called and said there was no hope. The cancer was too far gone.

I said make him comfortable, I'm coming to take him home. They let him walk out from the back. He saw me, and his tail started wagging. He kind of staggered to me. *Where've you been, Boss?*, he said.

ENDLESS OCTOBER

As I wrote this, he walked into my den and lay down at the foot of my desk. The drug patch for pain meds on his side and his shaved leg and bandaged other front leg all a testament to his last day in the hospital.

He was in his spot, I was in mine. I sat on the floor next to him and took his head in my lap. He gave me a huge sigh. "I'm tired," he said. "I love you, Boss."

"I love you, too, Ace. We are a good team."

His tail thumped the floor, and I cried.

(NSTRA CH Julia's FlyBoy Ace 03.10.2005-10.05.2015)

New Mexico, near Carlsbad Caverns

8. Old Roads

We see them, if we look. From old Southern wagon trails, sections now paved and named, running through green hills and long-abandoned plantation fields to depressions lined with oaks that shaded Sherman's troops on their March to the Sea. To Indian trails marked by the Signal Oaks, bent as they grew to mark trails and water holes and campsites. Even deep depressions made by hundreds of rolled tobacco bales making their way to the port cities of the Old South. In Western states, there are wagon trails with ruts still visible, and bridges with pilings showing just above creeks and streams with names like "Blood Creek" and "Muddy Stream." The Natchez Trace winds its way through hills and over fords of rivers and memories of resting stations with names like "She Boss Station" (named because the Indian man would point to the white woman and say "she boss") up in Tennessee. The ruts and indentations are still visible from the thousands of wagons struggling to the port city of Natchez, Mississippi. Ranches west of Old Man River and the Big Muddy, in family hands for hundreds of years, have gentle, sloping access roads carved out so that a team of horses could make the inclines to the "big house."

Usually, the old road is bypassed now, because we have hundreds of horses harnessed under the hood and brute force is the way of modern transport. We use huge machines go to straight up over the hills now. The old roads are dangerous and curvy and limit our speed, they say. Perhaps they are right, since the crosses marking tragedies are clustered on the curves.

In the Snake River valley of Idaho, narrow, gentle paths run from the caprock to the water, now disused and mostly forgotten.

In South Dakota, old wagon train trails are marked as points of interest; parts are paved since they are still the best way to get to Rapid City rapidly. All the trails have a gentle slope to convenience mule or ox-drawn transport.

The desert Southwest holds on to its old roads the longest, it seems. A lack of rain means tracks a hundred years old seem like they are merely disused and not totally abandoned. In New Mexico, after departing east from El Paso, the modern highway bulldozes its way across the bleak landscape until it hits the mountains and pushes its way up through peaks. The old roads are still visible, cut from the rocks, weaving back and forth, crossing old bridges, sometimes with a bit of paint still on the centerline – now fenced off, and employed as resting places for cows and coyotes.

Wisconsin and Minnesota, in the Great Northwoods, home to Paul Bunyan and Babe, the blue Ox, hide their old roads in new growth woods. They would follow the train tracks, rails now long gone, built to haul the huge trees to the sawmills in nearby mill towns. Some of the mills are still in operation. The roads are merely flat, gentle, overgrown depressions now, home to Ruffed Grouse, Elk, Bear, and Gray Wolf.

The western coast of Oregon, where towns were isolated except by boat, has roads carved into the cliffs above the crashing waves of the Pacific, in order to access their nearest neighbor up or down the coast. They are still visible when they are high enough to escape the constant scrubbing from the Pacific.

My kids grew up listening to me discuss three things on road trips: shortcuts, ridgelines, and old roads. All of them are related. Many old roads followed the crests of ridges (ridgelines) and were often the fastest way to get from place to place. Old Indian trails often followed the ridges. They were widened into roads, by settlers' wagons, and often were discovered as the best way for the railroads, who looked to avoid hills, and would always take the least incline possible.

I look at the old roads and wonder who traveled them, and why. Sometimes, it seems like such a waste to discard the work and sweat that went into their surveying and construction. But, I'm thinking those thoughts as I whiz by at a speed that covers a day's wagon train ride every 10 minutes. So, maybe I just answered my question.

Still, there is something sad about an old, cutoff piece of

road. We are saying to thousands of past travelers, "You went the wrong way. Look, this way is much faster!"

There's a sadness and dejection to an old road still winding through the trees or hanging on to the side of a mountain. "I've served my purpose, done my job, and now I'm set aside. Perhaps, they'll need me once again."

Perhaps. Or, like Route 66, it will be marked and remembered, from Chicago to Los Angeles, and celebrated by the children of the children who actually passed over the pavement in the family station wagon, the "way in back" seat facing rearward.

Keep an eye out for "the old roads." They are easiest to find out West, traveling through the mountains. And, when you find one, imagine an early automobile, or a wagon piled high with possessions, struggling up the hills, carrying a family wide-eyed with amazement at the scenic countryside so foreign to the land they left behind. Those old roads connected us. They made us a country.

Grouse woods near Phillips, Wisconsin

9. Dances with Wolves

Of the many species of grouse, the Ruffed Grouse is king. Ruffed Grouse are, arguably, the most difficult gamebird to even get into a position to shoot. Then, based on my amateur calculations, a hunter has one second (or less) after the flush to get a load of shot on the way!

With their range throughout the country, the best hunting, to my mind, is in the Northwoods: Wisconsin, Minnesota, and Michigan. The populations are large, the terrain is flat, and the available hunting land is plentiful and managed for grouse.

I've been a guest of the Northwoods for close to 15 years now. Every October, definitely, and every September, if I can, I load up the dogs for the annual trek to match wits with the finest gamebird on the planet.

A good, experienced grouse dog is a rare thing indeed. When I first began hunting in north central Wisconsin, I had

Rocket, a Brittany male, and Ruby, a setter female. Both were dead-broke dogs and took to the thick cover and trails of the Chequamegon National Forest with ease. They always checked in, never disappeared, rarely flushed birds, and were a real pleasure to hunt behind.

Over the years, those dogs passed on and my follow-on dogs were led by Julia's Bocephus (Bo). Bo was a Southern Quail Dog, bred and trained to "get on out there," locate coveys of quail and hold them, until I got there to flush and shoot.

That method of hunting is diametrically opposed to what a dog requires in Wisconsin. If a dog gets 100 yards from the hunter in the Wisconsin grouse woods (considered way too close for a quail dog), he was lost and of little use to a grouse hunter – the cover was simply too thick and the birds too skittish and too quick to flush.

Bo managed to do the job, but I was never at ease with him, even though he wore a beeper collar (pre-GPS days) to help me keep track of him and alert me to when he was on point. I would dread watching him head down into an alder swamp – and sure enough, his beeper would go off and I'd bust through the brush and muck to try and get to him in time to see the bird.

Many was the time, I would push my way through alders and briars and hemlock and fir trees for 50-60 yards and finally see Bo standing rock solid on point, only to hear the roar of the grouse wings just yards away and maybe get a glimpse of the gray ghost through the trees.

I tried for years to get Bo back into a comfortable grouse range, but I had trouble with the idea of really bearing down on him. I know some dogs that will adjust automatically – I owned one, my setter, Ruby – and they are such a pleasure. But, I have what I have and Bo and I came to a mutual understanding. He would work as close as he could, but I'd have to accept a little more effort on my part in the woods.

The limit to how many grouse can be harvested in one day is very liberal in Wisconsin. On a good year, a sojourn through the woods could get you numerous flushes in front, either side, or sometimes behind you; I counted those flushes but would not shoot. I made it a policy to not shoot at a bird unless it was over my pointed dog. (I know, that's crazy, my friends tell me.)

Getting a daily limit of Ruffed Grouse was never the goal. Working with my dogs to get that perfect series of point, flush, shot, and retrieve was the goal, and when I got several of those events in one day, I was completely satisfied.

However, Bo and I did happen to bump against the limit one time. Not many years ago, when Bo had some age on him and his legs started getting a little heavier, he stayed a lot closer. We were hitting trails we'd never seen before and exploring a little. One trail I remember in particular. A little northeast of Phillips,

Wisc., we discovered a little dashed line on the map and put out to take a look.

Bo worked out about thirty yards on either side of the trail that morning. I remember watching him and recalling other times and other trails and CRP fields – daydreaming on the pleasant walk through the forest. (Some days, when the sun is beating down on a warm September afternoon, grouse hunting consists of a pleasant, thoughtful saunter in the forest interrupted by a roaring freight train as a grouse flushes three feet from your ear!)

My thoughts were broken by his beeper off to my left. This time, I could actually see him when I looked through the alders and pines. He rarely false pointed, so I got excited when I moved quickly off the trail to a spot 10 yards in front of him. Two grouse blew out of the leafy, green grass and headed to Mexico. My old Fox 20 ga. hit my shoulder and I dropped the one to the left and Bo took off after it.

Right at that instant, four more birds flushed in a roar of wings to my right! I swung, saw the closest gray blur and let loose my second, and last, load of 7½'s.

The bird flew behind a fir tree just as I shot, but I cocked an ear and was rewarded with a dull thud as I heard the dead bird hit the forest floor.

Amazing! Six grouse on one point!

Bo brought the first bird back and I sent him for the second one. He located it with no help from me and put it in my hand. What a great start to the day! We managed to bag another single a little further up the old railroad bed.

Further on, I heard the noise from heavy machinery as we approached the old logging road, where I was parked at the head. I discovered that my little "two track" was being widened by the Forest Service. We popped out of the woods right in front of the biggest bulldozer I've ever seen! Bo and I were both impressed.

The driver must have been impressed with us, too, because he cut the engine and climbed down to chat. They are wonderful, friendly people are up there in Wisconsin, and the bulldozer operator was no exception. While we talked, I was in the middle of describing the six bird find Bo had earlier, when I noticed a curious look on his face as he glanced over my shoulder.

"You might want to take a look at your dog." he said and pointed behind me.

There was Bo, standing on the dirt berm thrown in to the woods by that monster machine. He was on point. I whispered, "Got to go" and jogged over to Bo, up the berm and down the other side, right into a flushing bird!

Four birds in the bag on one trail. That is a good day! On the way to the truck, perhaps a mile down the newly widened road,

ENDLESS OCTOBER

I found one more and we had our limit

I hunt alone a lot, but this is one time I really wanted to have a hunting partner so I could gloat a little bit. So, in lieu of that, the Old Knucklehead and I sat in the ferns by the truck and had a little love fest. I told him how good he was, and he allowed as to how I was trainable.

Last year, I was introducing some friends to the North-woods. I would point to a trail head for them to hunt in the morn-ing, tell them where I was going to be, wish them luck and agree to meet for lunch, or, failing that, dinner back at the motel.

As luck would have it, the warm fall day started turning dark a little early, and it was almost black by noon. The rain started as a sprinkle and then gradually got worse.

We put out on a trail that had produced a lot of birds over the years. I was the only one on it and I determined that a little rain wasn't going to interfere with a grouse hunt. I did swap my guns out, though, and the little Fox went back into the case, replaced by a 20-ga. SKB Model 100 I used for weather like this.

Bo and I started down the trail with him running ahead, then he would veer off to a side. And, then, he was gone. I walked and whistled and listened for his beeper for an hour. The rain was heavy at times but merely a downpour at others. He could have been 20 yards out in the thick growth, on point, and I would not have heard or seen him.

Finally, I returned to the truck, dried off, cleaned, dried and oiled and cased the gun, put on some dry clothes and headed out to find my dog. The trail was about 3 miles long, meaning 6 miles, out and back.

It was getting darker now and I was getting a little more concerned about the old boy. The good thing was the temperature was quite warm – in the 60s. If he did have to spend the night in the woods, I was sure he would be able find a dry spot and stay warm.

Walking, whistling, listening, and bouncing between anger and concern as I walked down the trail, I rounded a bend as the trail dropped off sharply. I stood for a minute listening and staring down the trail.

Suddenly, a big gray shape stepped out on the trail about 30 yards away. He was looking down the trail, away from me. After a second or two, I recognized him as a Gray Wolf. Instantly, I realized he and I were looking for the same thing. I was looking for my old, bird hunting companion. This big, gray boy was looking for dinner, and it downright pissed me off!

"Hey" I yelled, "Get out of here!" (Or words to that effect.)

I expected him to jump and run like the coyotes I'd encountered numerous times out West. His reaction was quite a bit different from what I anticipated. That huge, majestic canine slowly turned his head to the right and looked directly in the eye. Then, he slowly turned back to the left and trotted down the center of the trail without so much as a backward glance.

Even now, I'm impressed with him. He was huge – easily three times the size of my bird dogs, which would make him more than 120 pounds! And as he trotted off, in the direction of my lost dog, he more glided that ran.

Just then, I came to the realization that I was completely unarmed! It was one of the few times in my life I really did want a gun in my hands – and it was resting, dry and well oiled, in my truck more than a mile away.

Not thinking all that clearly and remembering the literature I'd read about wolves not bothering humans (yeah, except for the thousands of years of history and stories about wolves devouring little kids and old men ... the big, bad, wolf, and on and on ...), so I pressed on down the trail calling and keeping a careful eye behind me.

An hour later, at the end of the trail, I turned and headed back to the truck. Concern now was for my ability to make it back before dark. I picked up the pace.

Head down in the rain and moving quickly, I rounded a bend and there he was. A 35-pound bundle of shaking, wet Setter!

I'm not sure who was happier to see the other, but I got down on my knees and hugged that mutt and thanked Jesus for, again, answering my prayers.

We didn't stay long on that trail in the rain, and I put him on a lead and headed out. He was so exhausted, he tried to lie down a few times and, finally, I had to pick him up and throw him over my shoulders. We needed to get out of those woods – now!

The sun was long gone behind thick clouds and darkness was settling in. The GPS said we had more than a mile of up and down to go. I remembered that song from the '60s, "He ain't heavy, he's my brother ..." as I carried him up and down hills, slipping on the up-slopes with rain dripping down my neck and wet dog scent in my nose.

Song or not, don't believe it: he got heavy as this old man got close to the road. I put him down and we finished side by side, both of us limping and panting hard.

Back at the motel, I checked the old campaigner over for cuts, bruises, and ticks. It was then I noticed blood on my hands, when I ran them over his haunches. I turned him around and gave him a closer inspection. On his right rear leg, just below the tail, was the perfectly round hole.

Bo wasn't talking, but to this day I think he encountered my big, gray friend, too. I think we were being watched during our lit-

ENDLESS OCTOBER

tle reunion on the trail, in the rain, in the Wisconsin grouse woods.

RANDY SCHULTZ

**Randy with Blue Quail in New Mexico
(Photo by Tim Bartlett)**

10. Lessons Learned

One of the benefits of traveling and hunting is the chance to see all types of terrain and species of upland birds, meet all kinds of farmers, ranchers, bird hunters, and land owners.

But, no matter where I am, what state, no matter which dogs are in the back of whatever Beast I'm driving, no matter who I'm with (or by myself), there are a few rules to live by. Some are hard-won lessons. I will admit, I was on the wrong end of these rules occasionally. A wise man said it's smart to learn from your mistakes, but it's wise to learn from the mistakes of others. There is no sense in merely remembering and adapting if the only one to benefit is you. So, here are a few items I think are important. Some of these items are self-explanatory; some will need a little background. All of them will keep you out of trouble.

1.) Never. Ever. Go back and hunt an area shown to you by another hunter without their express, absolute consent. "He knew that's where I was going" or "It's public land; anyone can hunt there" or "There's someone's truck there" are no good. Taking another hunter to a spot is a trust between bird hunters. If he shows you a spot, you are forbidden from going back unless he gives you the OK. If you can't live with that, don't go. You'll lose a friend.

2.) Leave gates as you found them, wide open or secure. In fact, match the knot on the rope, if you can. This is a BIG deal!

3.) Always compliment another man's dog. If you denigrate his dog, you just cussed his wife, or worse. Be prepared for the unpleasant consequences. There is at least one thing every dog does well. Notice what it is and compliment him ("Old Jake can really turn sharp chasing those pheasant!"), and the hunter. Also, maybe more important, don't ever touch another man's dog without permission. God help you if you strike or kick at another man's dog. If you are one of those guys who just can't keep from "giving training advice to help the dog," learn to keep your advice to yourself.

4.) If both of you shoot the same bird, assume you missed, tell your buddy, "Nice shot!" Let him carry the bird. I've seen new hunters swell with pride over their "first" pheasant (or other gamebird) that way.

5.) Hunting private land? Tell the owner if he needs help, for any reason, you can lend a hand. I've unstuck trucks, put in fence posts, rounded up cows, and put out fires. It's the friendly thing to do.

6.) Don't shoot over the limit. Know the rules and stay within them. Be polite and friendly to Game Wardens and local law enforcement. They have a tough job. When I see one, I break down my gun and get my papers out. I don't wait to be asked. I think they appreciate it. Then, ask them where the birds are.

7.) Eat in local cafes. Every town has one and each one has a group of local farmers/ranchers that meet around sunrise to drink coffee and solve problems. They usually are friendly and are wondering what the new guy (you) is doing in town. I've met and befriended numerous people by just explaining I drove all the way from Georgia to hunt the local bird.

8.) When the day is done, the order in which items are completed should conform to the old Cavalry saying: *The horse, the saddle, the man.* Take care of your dog, first and foremost! Clean his feet and check him for stickers and wounds. Check his eyes for seeds. Feed and water him. Make sure he has warm, dry bedding, etc. Then, clean your gun, boots, chaps, truck. Put all your electronics on chargers, write important stuff in your logbook before you forget it. Check fuel and water on board for tomorrow. Then, after all that other stuff, take care of yourself. Keep the order in order. Remember to keep the main thing the main thing!

9.) Get a puppy when your youngest dog hits five years old. You will always have one in his prime, one old, wizened veteran, and a young pup in the string.

10.) Field Trials and Hunt Tests are simulations of the real thing. Don't look down your nose at the real thing. Do the real thing every chance you can. *The best dog that ever walked the face of this planet never smelled a pen-raised bird, ran a course, or was judged.* Get your nose out of the air, suck it up and let your dog fulfill its genetic destiny. I know, it's scary thinking about letting your dog off the lead! Ask for help. Start with baby steps, ask some folks who have hunted how to get started.

11.) Dogs get hurt, cut, snake bit, lost, quilled, tired, cold, wet, hot, cranky, etc. Have a plan and a first aid kit on hand. Carry a multi-tool, tape, blood stop. Have the local vet number in your phone. See number 10, above. A dog's getting hurt is not a common occurrence, but it does happen. Don't let it keep you from letting your dog do what it is meant to do.

12.) Keep the dogs warm at night. Every calorie a dog doesn't use staying warm is a calorie it can use to recover from the day's exertions. Put a heater in the back of the truck or trailer, or, better yet, let them have their own pillow on the bed!

13.) Let your yes mean yes and your no mean no. No need to swear an oath.

14.) Buy good equipment, learn to use it, take care of it. Nothing is less impressive than an expensive gun dragged through the briars.

15.) Plan, plan, plan. Call DNR, call people who know people. Do not expect anyone to hand over hard-won information about hunting spots. They've been driving to and hunting the area for years. Why should they tell you anything? If they do, be grateful! You haven't "paid your dues" so don't expect a handout.

16.) Put a set of chains in your truck. You might be able to drive WAY back in on frozen ground. Coming out on thawed-out snot may be more problematic. A good set of chains or other traction device is good to have. You might not need one for years, but when you need them, nothing else will do. Take a sleeping bag in the truck. An overnight is sometimes unavoidable. Might as well be comfortable.

17.) Take time to get where you are going. It's better to get there rested than gutting it out and taking two days to recover.

18.) Remember why you do this. Pass along what you know. Take a kid hunting.

11. Fences

I hate barbed-wire fences. I have two nice scars on my right leg. One is a long and jagged gash on the inside of my knee – from Texas. My dog was on point and I needed to cross a barbed-wire fence in a hurry. It was a new and substantial fence, and, going over, I stumbled and felt some pain, but the fence let go, and I made it across in good order. I kicked up the covey and got a double, as I recall. (Hey, it's my "recall." I can recall anything I want.)

A few minutes later, my right boot got wet and squishy. "Odd!" I thought. "I haven't been through any creeks!"
A quick check revealed a nice gash about three inches long and, by now, a half-inch wide. That night, I put some EMT Gel in the wound and wrapped it up. A couple of weeks later, I was good as new. The second one is from Nebraska and a similar, though less gory, situation.

Crossing a barbed-wire fence is always problematic. Most can be stepped over by pushing down on the top wire. Failing that, rolling under the bottom wire might work. Or, stepping up the wire, near a post, like a ladder. All of these choices have their own special danger. Straddling barbed wire, while expedient, puts tender parts of male (and female) anatomy close to sharp metal spikes. Rolling under puts the bird hunter down in the dirt with sandspurs. And, climbing wire over a metal post just sounds dangerous. (It is, and I have another scar on my stomach to prove it!).

My story continues in a remote part of Arizona, not far from the Mexico border, in the search for Mearns Quail. My friend Wally and I were hunting a hilly, rock-strewn area with grass and oaks, the preferred habitat of the Mearns. My GPS alerted me to my dog, Ruby, pointing a covey of Mearns Quail about 150 yards away, slightly to the left. As luck would have it, just across a tight, new, shiny barbed-wire fence.

Normally, I approach fences in a deliberate manner, searching for low spots, gates, broken top strands, etc. When a dog is pointed on the other side, my thought processes go from thoughtful and deliberate to "get your butt over there!"

I approached the fence, pushed down on the top wire, and swung my left foot over the top. At that point, my shoelace caught the wire as my boot crossed over. I was hung up half-way across! Attempting to extricate myself, I pulled my boot back over, hoping the shoelace would unhook. (All the while checking my Alpha to make sure Ruby was still pointed.) The shoelace was stuck fast, wrapped around the barbed-wire strand. The situation was this: I was standing on one leg, holding a shotgun in my left hand, barbed-wire fence in my right hand, with my left leg affixed to the fence. And, I began to fall backwards ...

There are many things a man in my situation could be thinking at this point. I, in my infinite wisdom, was thinking, "I hope Wally isn't seeing this!" (Which reminds of the "Attack Pilot's Prayer": *Lord, please don't let me screw up. But, if I do, please don't let anyone see it.*)

As I began to topple backwards, I raised my left hand to save my old Fox, and gripped the fence tighter with my right to perhaps slow or stop my slide to the rocks under my right foot. I'm still amazed at how fast a body can pick up speed (32 feet per second squared) and equally amazed at how quickly it can stop when it hits Arizona rock.

Just as I hit with my vest supplies impacting my lower back, my left foot released and I was sprawled out on my back, left arm up (gun secured!), right hand still gripping the fence – and stunned. I wanted to laugh, but it hurt. Just then I heard the covey flush and, louder yet, my hunting partner stay conspicuously silent.

After I managed to cross the fence on the second attempt, we failed to find the birds, and, much more to my chagrin, my fence-crossing abilities were no longer a subject of speculation, but a matter of record.

Dang, my back hurts. I hate fences.

Randy Schultz with his eager partner, Bo.

Bocephus, known as Bo

12. Bo's Big Trial

In March of 2001, I received an invitation to enter Bo in the Quail Unlimited National Championship in Bronwood, Georgia. He was a little more than 2 years old and we were at the end of the hunting season. We'd been all over the country, Arizona, Wisconsin, North Dakota, South Dakota, Oklahoma, Texas, Kansas, and Nebraska, hunting anything and everything that flew and could be pointed.

In addition, Bo had been field trialing some, on and off, when we could get time on the weekend. The entry fee was pretty stiff, but this one was close to home and they had some great prizes to the winners. I figured Bo could run with any dog on a good day, so we entered the trial.

The "beat your bracemate" format meant you would only need to outscore the dog/handler you were running against in your 30-minute brace in order to advance to the next round. This meant after every round half the field advanced, or didn't, and it only took a few days to cut the field down to one dog, from more than a hundred.

I was thankful Bo wasn't intimidated by the level of competition at the event, because I certainly was. I met handlers and dogs who were only words on paper up until then. These were "the big boys" – professionals in every sense of the word.

There were dogs with ten and twenty NSTRA Championships and handlers that did nothing but travel the country to enter these dogs in major field trials. They had motor homes dragging all stainless steel dog trailers with All Terrain Vehicles loaded on top. And, they all knew each other.

Conversations typically made reference to the "that Champion of Champions Trial" or "the Quail Invitational Trial," or just "Amo" (where the biggest trials were held in Amo, Indiana).

Not only was I an outsider to the conversation, but I had no idea what in the world these guys were talking about. "Bo, we are in a heap of trouble here, boy! I'm pretty sure we bit off more than we can chew!" I'd mutter. Bo just smirked and curled up to get some rest.

I remember the very first brace we ran in that major trial – on a huge, flat, square field. The gallery, as the on-lookers were called, could see everything and there were plenty of comments, both complimentary and not.

A field trialer's nightmare was to really mess up in front of the gallery – maybe miss the bird on the rise, or have the dog run right over the bird without pointing. The hoots and catcalls would travel for what seemed miles as the peanut gallery would get their licks in while they could. And the better you were known, the more fun at your expense.

Of course, some of it was meant in jest. It was acknowledged as a time to get even between the "big boys" and it seemed the bird handler, as the guy who put the quail in the field was called, would always put one somewhere right in front of the gallery. Bo and I had an early brace and there was still a chill in the air. It was cool, but humid, and that was good for the dog's ability to scent the birds.

Bo was likely to strike scent a fair ways off from the bird, I realized, and that meant we should be OK in finding birds. Of course, the "beat your bracemate" format meant our competition had the same advantages. It simply boiled down to outscoring the other dog over the next thirty minutes.

We were nervous, waiting in the little area called the "blind," while the bird handler set out five more birds after the previous brace finished. I don't remember my bracemate, but I do remember stroking Bo's head and making small talk about the weather and scenting and how the opponent's dog looked real tough and "I hope you guys will take it easy on this old country dog!"

It was the usual talk, trying to appear cool, calm, and unaffected by the situation. An unknown, I really had an advantage because they didn't know me or my dog. It was assumed we were one of the local meat dogs that entered just because we wanted to get out of the house. It was also assumed we would be eliminated in the first round. To be sure, I wasn't certain that assumption wasn't correct. I really did feel out of my league – although I had perfect confidence in Bo.

After the birds were hidden, we were called out ("Bring 'em out!") and went to the start line with dogs pulling in eagerness and judges waiting. We stood apart at the line waiting for the start and the head judge called down from his horse, "Everyone ready? Turn 'em loose!"

I slipped Bo's lead and he took off like a shot – full stride, it seemed, in three or four steps! He veered to the left, while the other dog went right. That was good. I didn't want the other dog trying to foot-race Bo around the field. I took two or three steps into the field to follow him, loading my gun and watching his progress at the same time. Suddenly, he spun around and locked up in classic Bo fashion: body twisted, tail at the 10 o'clock position, legs spread to support himself, and head absolutely still. He went from what seemed a hundred miles an hour to zero in the blink of an eye!

We were only 10 seconds into this thing and Bo was already on a bird! I yelled "Point!" as the adrenaline surged, and I walked quickly to his front, checking the position of the judge, gallery and other handler and dog. I consciously noted the direction of the breeze, realizing the bird would be upwind of the dog's nose, and I headed for that spot. I was about 20 feet from Bo when the ground moved and a whir of wings came up from a clump of grass and headed out away from us. I shouldered my gun and pulled the trigger while watching the bird. It kept flying! I shot again, but now the bird was in full fight and a long ways off. I missed! The first bird on the first day of the biggest trial I've ever been in and I missed the bird!

I shook my head, as the gallery crowed, and watched Bo chase that bird all the way across the field – maybe a third of a mile. The rules don't say you must kill the bird, only that the dog must retrieve the bird. Bo chased that bird down, found it, gently picked it up and ran back to me with an unhurt bird in his mouth. He put it in my hand with a disgusted look and took off again.

All I could do was act calm and remark to the judge what a good retrieve that was and he laughed a little as took the bird out of my hand. "Amazing how these little birds can fly with all that lead shot in them, isn't it?" he remarked grinning.

I did notice the gallery was very complimentary of Bo and his retrieve, though. "Maybe we can salvage this." I thought, as I watched Bo cover the field.

The rest of the brace flashed by; we managed to have three birds to our opponent's two and we beat him on points. We advanced and he went home. Only half the dogs returned the next day. Win or go home is brutal and fair. I knew every time we took to the field we could be heading home in thirty minutes. To advance we would need to win twice this day.

The next brace was in a different field with lots of trees and cut corn, lots of little ins and outs and hills. It was a lot like the kind of hunting we'd been doing all year. I felt very comfortable from the time I left the line. One thing a dog must demonstrate to win a major trial is the ability to "back" or honor another dog's point. He does that by pointing himself at the other dog. In bird hunting, this is a very useful trait since occasionally the pointing dog will be out of sight in bush or swamp, etc. His hunting mate might see him and will "back" him. Now, the hunter may see the "backing" dog and finally find the pointing dog and the birds.

I never did work Bo a lot on backing, but during the second run an opportunity presented itself, and I called Bo in so he could see the pointing dog and back him. He flew around the corner, responding to my whistle, saw the other dog and skidded to a stop! It wasn't fancy or elegant. It was a back – pure and simple – and it satisfied the requirement. In the unlikely event we made it to the finals, the judges would be checking the scores to make sure Bo had demonstrated at least one back during the trial.

We were tied at two birds apiece and both of us had a back, also. My opponent was a good friend and professional trainer with a great dog. But, here we were, tied up with fifteen more minutes to find another bird in the field. We worked along the edges of the field, hoping to catch a bird either heading for the shade of the trees, or a bird walking back onto the field.

As we moved around the back of the field, alongside a row of pine trees, Bo was in full flight along the mowed lane that was the boundary of the field. If he was standing in the mowed lane when he pointed a bird, he would be considered "out of bounds" and the find would not count, even if the bird was "in bounds." I whistled a command to turn and he immediately jerked left back into a clump of tall grass that was in bounds. As I watched, he never came out the other side! "Point" yelled the judge from his vantage point on top of his horse.

Adrenaline shot through me as I checked the area for safety and eased into the clump of tall grass looking for Bo. There he was- frozen on point. His eyes were glazed and his breathing was fast! Intense! I kicked the grass in front of him and a big, fat quail shot up and headed out to the pines for safety. The gun was on my shoulder and fired before I remembered doing it and the bird crumpled dead to the ground.

As soon as I shot, Bo released from the point and, when the

bird hit the ground, Bo was only five yards away from him. He snatched up the bird and ran back to put it into my hand. Three birds on the card now, with a back, too. Bo had done it one more time and we advanced to the third day. The dog was on a roll, the shooting was better, and the "luck factor" was most definitely in our favor. Every trialer knows ability and good nose and perfect training can only go so far. Eventually, choices have to be made: "do I turn right or left, turn back or head on?"

I always figured, for field trialing, about 60 percent was the dog, 25 percent was the handler and 15 percent was blind luck. This weekend, this day, this trial, we were firing on all cylinders. Bo was on fire, my shooting was perfect, we were working as a team and every decision we made paid off.

At the end of second run on the final day, only four dogs were left. Nervously, we endured another drawing to determine the order of the last two braces – the highest scoring dog would win.

Bo and I drew the second brace, so we would run after the first two dogs finished. We were drawn against a dog that was in-credibly talented. He was a German Shorthair Pointer, a mature male, and these were his home grounds. It was a tough draw, but I knew we would have a small advantage. Our opponent did not like briars. This 80-acre field was mostly broomsedge grass, but there were some really nice areas in the interior of the field that were sprinkled with a low growing briar.

On the other hand, he was fast, smart, and very knowledge-able about the fields. The first brace with two very powerful English Setters took off for one hour in the double-sized field. For the finals, the field size was doubled and twice the number of birds were hidden.

After running five previous times, this last brace, for the championship, was a test of endurance for the dogs, as well. These two hit the field as if they had been resting all day! The level of competition in a national trial is on a plane far above the local trial – all the dogs (and most handlers) are polished professionals by the time they get to a "big one."

The first brace dogs covered every square inch of the field with speed and class. Bo and I couldn't watch. We went behind some cars and sat down and pondered how in the world we managed to get to the finals. I came to the conclusion that sometimes men are successful in spite of themselves, rather than because of anything they do. Bo wasn't talking.

Every shot increased my concern. At the completion of the two braces, after all four dogs had run, it was the final scores that counted. Bo and I were running not only against our bracemate, but against the two dogs currently on the field, as well. The tension in the gallery was high. Men and women talked in low voices and even the wives and friends of the competitors on the field were reserved. It reminded me a little of a funeral.

ENDLESS OCTOBER

The weather was beautiful. It was about forty degrees with a little breeze from the south and puffy clouds and bright blue sky. The broomsedge, a tall, brown grass the original settlers used to tie in bunches and sweep out the cabins, was moving with the breeze.

One of the setters in the first brace swung by the gallery and, within the blink of an eye, froze on point – the breeze ruffling the long hair on his vertical tail. He was a beautiful dog and I admired him, as his handler flushed the bird and shot. The dog's retrieve was equally flawless – right to hand with speed and class. "We are in over our heads, Bo!" I muttered.

Bo still wasn't talking.

The first brace ended after an hour. One dog found and scored four birds and also was scored for a back. The other found four birds, but was not scored with a back. Out of ten birds hidden in the field, only eight were found. According to the rules, another ten birds were put out, regardless. That was good for us, but we still had to find the birds and, then, beat our bracemate.

We took to the blind like we'd been doing this all our lives. A little "devil may care" saunter was thrown in there for good measure. I gave a wink to my friends wishing me good luck – as if to say "No luck needed today, my friends. This one's in the bag!"

Inside, it was a different story. The fact that I kept checking my pockets to make sure I had shells, whistle, shotgun, and dog seemed to be lost on everyone but Bo. When we sat down in the blind, he sat quietly by my knee and put his head on my leg and looked right at me. "Calm down, boss. All you need to do is shoot them; I'll do the rest!"

My bracemate and his dog sat a few feet away. While this was the handler's first final, his dog had been here many times. So, I asked him to at least leave one bird for me and my broke down dog and wished him "Good Luck."

The Head Judge yelled, "Bring 'em out!" and we both left the blind for the start line. I was on autopilot but Bo was fired up. He pulled and jumped and twisted as I walked to the line. I stared hard at the field, looking for movement, anything to gain an advantage at the last second.

The breeze was about ten mph from the left so I lined up to the left. When we released the dogs, any bird upwind of Bo would send scent right to him first. I learned a long time ago to take care of the little things I could control – lining up was one of them.

We stood at the line, held our dogs by the collar, and waited for word to start. The judges were astride their horses behind us and I could hear them discussing which dog they would ride behind and score. I heard Jimmy, a National Judge and the Head Judge, say he would take the setter (Bo) while the other judge, equally qualified, would take the shorthair. They rode up behind us and Jimmy asked, "Handlers ready?"

We nodded and he yelled, "Turn 'em loose!"

We both released our dogs and off they went.

The shorthair sprinted out front and stayed in a straight line with Bo only a few feet behind him. After about 20 yards of that, I whistled and Bo cut to the right and headed back to me. Suddenly, the shorthair spun around locked up like a statue! "Point!" the handler yelled.

"You got it!" the judge answered.

As the other handler walked to his dog, I had a choice. Should I leave the scene and try to find another bird while my opponent was tied up with his find, or should I bring Bo in for a back and the lesser points associated with that? Bo made the decision for me when he looked to his right, saw the other dog on point, and stopped to a point himself. "Back!" I yelled and walked over to Bo to take his collar and hold him while the other handler flushed and shot his bird for the retrieve.

Bo looked good. I could tell he would listen to me today, and that was a good feeling. Some days, you could see wildness in his eyes. When I saw that, I knew he was going to be a handful. But, today, he looked all business. Bo was a bird dog with birds in front of him – an animal in the situation for which he was bred and trained. This was the "perfect storm" – all the hard work, hunting, genetics and situational training came to focus on this day and time. Right here- right now.

It doesn't happen often, but when it does, it's a beautiful thing. The other dog completed his work and the judge told me to turn Bo loose. As I did, I started walking to the left, into the wind and towards the larger part of the field. Bo flew by me, moving back and forth and maximizing the amount of area he covered with his nose.

Remembering what an old bird hunter told me, "Son, a bird dog is nothing more than a life support system for his nose!", I tried to put Bo in a position to work upwind as much as I could. On a day like today, he could scent a bird thirty yards away, if he was downwind of it. He was fast; he quickly worked out of sight in the tall grass. I followed his progress by watching the judge on horse-back. The judge stopped, raised his arm and shouted "Point!"

Bo had his first bird, but he was two hundred yards away. I picked up the pace to get to him and not waste any time. By the time I got there, I was out of breath and sweat was running in to my eyes. I was thinking I'd never see the bird if it got up. I scanned the area to make sure the shot would be safe and then I stepped in front of Bo.

The bird exploded out to my right and the gun was on my shoulder and the bird dropped. Bo was on it the second it hit the ground and delivered it to me, dropped it into my hand and took off to the back corner of the field; one down.

Then, I heard a shot from the front of the field – down two to one! I can picture the day like it was yesterday with the blue sky and white puffy clouds. Spring in the South can be really pretty – once you get past the weather extremes and tornadoes.

The breeze was blowing from the south and it was still cool and dry with just enough humidity for the dogs. Part of the field was planted in sorghum strips with a few rows of three- or four-year-old planted pines. There was a section along a bottom that held some stunted oaks with large patches of a low-growing briar.

Along the other end, the field bordered a pine forest. All this was separated from the surrounding land by a plowed strip of land perhaps 12 feet wide. (Bo competed enough to know that when he reached a plowed strip, he would turn and head back into the field. Some dogs never figured that out and the frustration was evident in the handler's voice trying to get them back on the field.)

The gallery disappeared. I would think of where Bo had been and where we needed to go next. I would watch the judge, Bo, the other dog, when he was in sight and the other handler's orange when he wasn't, and always head for ground not yet swept by that nose.

The hour passed by so quickly, I was sure there was a mistake. After twenty minutes, we had two more birds – three now. I knew we needed at least five on the scorecard to have a chance.

RANDY SCHULTZ

We already had the scored back. Five finds and a back would beat the first two dogs and, I hoped, our bracemate.

I started working Bo around the edges of the field. Typically, the birds will walk away from the commotion in the center of an area. Eventually, they will reach the edge up against the plowed strip. They won't want to expose themselves to hawks, so they will stay in the grass along the edges. We were in the downwind, northwest, corner of the field, when I turned into the wind and started along the edge.

I whistled Bo along with me, and he fell right into the routine – hunting from the plowed strip back in to the field about thirty yards then back to the strip. We moved along, into the wind, hoping we'd made the right decision. "Point" I yelled!

Bo was working back from the strip into the field, when he spun around and froze. Yes! It was working! Bo had a big, fat, male quail pinned down. The flush, shot, and retrieve were classic and we were on our way again – four birds on the card.

We combed the edge for another half-mile and found another bird in the southwest corner of the huge field. This one was in the last little piece of grass before he was safe out of bounds. But the bird counted and Bo had five birds!

We had ten minutes left and we were a long way from the start line and gallery. I could see the trucks in the distance and barely see a few folks watching with binoculars, I thought. I knew that every shot would bring the question, "How many has he got now? How about the shorthair – how many for him?"

We worked along the short southern boundary and then turned north to the gallery. We had only about five minutes left, now. I was trying to remember, in my concentration, if I'd heard any shots from my bracemate – and I couldn't remember hearing any. I was concentrating so hard on my own handling that I blocked out the other stuff.

I asked the judge about it when he was close enough to me, but he couldn't remember either. I knew the trial was over for us, as we walked to the finish and the last few minutes ticked down. We'd done all we could do. My raggedy old knot-head setter, my school dropout, and I had done our best.

I chatted with Jimmy, the judge, and relaxed as we covered the last few yards waiting for the final seconds to pass. Point! Bo swung around and locked up! He wasn't 10 feet from the boundary and two ladies talking about the long drive back to Indiana!

"Time!" yelled the judge.

I was allotted one minute, in this situation, to finish my work and get a score. I quickly moved to Bo. He was twisted like a pretzel just in front of the gallery – wound tighter than a coiled spring and, I swear, he had a grin on his face! This was the "money bird" – I knew it, the crowd knew it, and my bracemate, who was just coming off the field, knew it.

I kicked the clump of grass five feet in front of Bo's nose and out the quail came! He flew straight at the ladies from Indiana – they screamed and dropped to the ground – worried about a load of birdshot.

I yelled, "Safety" and let Bo chase the bird through the gallery and into the woods beyond. I let him go, knowing with six birds and a back on the scorecard, we had just won the big one – the 2001 Quail Unlimited National Championship!

Bo came back with the bird, unhurt, in his mouth and handed him to me. "We're not quitting yet, are we? There's still daylight left!"

Every dog has his day, they say. Bo had his in Bronwood, Georgia.

Randy and Blue in New Mexico

13. A Day in the Life: Hunting Blue Quail

The rains came on time and in quantity. Southeastern New Mexico was awash in grass, Cowpen Daisy, Sunflowers, mesquite, shin-oak and, now, Blue Quail. According to the harvest we took throughout the week, I can say there was more than one hatch, as well. Some birds we took were very small due to a later hatch. Multiple hatches would explain the significant increase in bird numbers.

Driving the local roads in the oil patch, I dropped off the cap down into some of the nicest-looking habitat I'd seen all week. The day was cool and clear and one could see all the way in to next week.

Cowpen Daisy, Sunflower, mesquite, grass, sand – all combined to make this a quail heaven.

Quickly, I pulled in to a pump-jack location and grabbed Ruby to put boots on her to protect her feet from the sand spurs. I parked and walked around to the back of the truck, dropped the tailgate and, immediately, out of a mesquite bush 50 feet from the truck, 30 Blue Quail flushed out and flew 50 yards to another bush. Many more ran out of the bush following the initial, flying crowd.

Trying to put boots on a dog in a hurry is problematic, at best. Hurrying to boot a dog that's seen 30 birds flush 50 feet away is pretty close to impossible! They can move their legs, feet, bodies in ways I'd never thought possible!

Finally, we got it done, and Ruby and I started west toward the flushed covey. Almost immediately, she pointed, smelling the covey remains. I honored her point and kicked around a bit, I reached over to her, tapped her on the head and said, "OK, girl, let's go find 'em."

We worked up to the next shrub. Up the dunes, over the top, and out in to the flat loaded with Daisies and grass. What a perfect place, I thought! For 20 minutes, Ruby hunted hard and came up with nothing. I started south, thinking they might have run toward some bigger dunes. Ruby picked up on my idea and dropped into the dune bottoms. She spun around just as the covey flushed up and over the top, heading west.

We drank some water, and conspired and commiserated for a few minutes. Finally, I turned her loose again and up over the dune she went after the covey.

Climbing sand dunes is a great aerobic exercise, and, as I got to the top and looked out on a flat area with mesquite bushes and lots of grass, I paused for a minute to catch my breath. Also, I saw a dog on point. Ruby was locked up on a mesquite bush about 100 yds away.

I moved as fast as I could to get to her, but, when I was about 40 yards away, the covey flushed again, going farther west. I saw some of them land on the top of another dune about 100 yards away, and some more cross a fence and dive in to a mesquite bush about the same distance away.

Ruby took off after them, as I trudged through the sand and shin-oak, gun ready, looking for singles. Deciding to cross the fence and trap the mesquite bush crowd, I found a low area in the substantial fence, and stepped over the top. I hurried to Ruby, again on point, at the mesquite. "Gotcha now, you little buggers!" I thought.

Lots of tracks and a locked-down bird dog will get me excited any day, but they eluded us again. They were gone, leaving only tracks. I began to think these sly, desert runners had seen a dog before!

I turned her loose once again, and we started working the area making long loops through the grass and mesquite. We would go way downwind and turn back into the wind and crisscross along looking for scent.

Finally, we got back to the fence and bush. I called her in and we headed to the dune where half the covey had landed. It was another dry hole.

In the distance, we could hear the birds whistling and gathering up again and heading back to the truck where we flushed them originally. Ruby was dry and I was out of water by this time, and getting a little weary. "C'mon, girl," I said. "Let's head back and find another covey."

I came to the fence. It was a new, tight, and shiny fence

with good wire and there was no way I could step over it. I stepped on the bottom strand, right up against the metal fencepost, and started to heave myself over when the fence link broke, and I slid down on top of the post. I had a lot of gear on and that probably protected me, but the top of that post hit me in the stomach and slid up my chest.

I jumped back, took off my glove and felt the area to see if I was bleeding. Even though it hurt, no blood showed. Good to go! Finally, I dug a hole in the sand and braved sand-burrs by rolling under the fence. Coming up the other side, I walked off after my dog.

Ruby came to me again for a drink. I put my gun down and took out every bottle I had to give her the last few drops. We were about a mile from the truck, had four covey flushes (three pointed) and no birds/no shots.

I rubbed her head a bit, and then I sent her on, put on my gloves, picked up my gun and looked ahead to where we were going. I was thinking about the wind direction, truck location, etc. My first step took me directly into a three-foot-high Cholla Cactus bush!

Cholla Cactus is bad when you know it's in the area. It is even worse when you have no idea it's around and it hits your leg from ankle to belt! Of course, I wasn't wearing chaps that day.

I put my gun down, took off my vest, dropped my pants, and started pulling spines from my leg and thigh until I couldn't feel any more sticking out.

As long as I was half naked, I checked out my fence-post scrape and it wasn't too bad. There were no gashes, at any rate.

I looked around and noticed there was ONE Cholla bush as far as the eye could see, and it was three feet from me – I've always been lucky like that. Just then, Ruby's collar alert went off. She was on point 256 yards from me in a mesquite mound area.

I made it to her in time for another covey rise, and I finally dropped two birds for good retrieves. One bird ran down a hole. By the time I got there, Ruby was up to her shoulders with sand flying everywhere and she came out with the bird in her mouth!

We worked singles for about 30 minutes, generally heading in the direction of the truck. I dropped a few more quail over her points. Finally, I reached for some shells and came up dry. I had two shells in my gun, the sun was getting low, the temperature was dropping, we were out of water. and the truck wasn't too far away. "Here, Ruby, let's get back to the truck. Good girl!"

She worked ahead of me into a flat grassy area and locked up again on a patch of grass. Two birds got up and flew directly in to the lowering sun! I shot twice. I thought I could see them well enough. but, somehow, they kept on going, apparently unhurt. (I know. I'm as amazed as you.)

Worse, I was out of shells with an empty gun. And, for the next 10 minutes, Ruby would point a clump of grass, and I would kick a few birds in the air to watch them fly off. Laughing, I scratched her ears and loved on her as we headed to the truck. "Ruby," I told her, "nice job, girl!" It was an average cast on an average day in the desert Blue Quail country.

Hunting Blue Quail can bring out the best and worst in a man. Generally, the best, I think.

I have no idea why I like that smelly, prickly, sandy, hot, cold, windy, piece of dirty Southeastern New Mexico, but I do.

**Randy, Shack, and pheasant in North Dakota
(Photo by BJ Schultz)**

14. Hunting the Blizzard

They don't even call them blizzards any more. In North Dakota, they are called "major winter weather events." With the right clothing and a good attitude, bad weather hunting can be very enjoyable. My LL Bean hunting pants were waterproof, windproof, and very light. I did not even wear long underwear. My Orvis wool Elmer Fudd hat, or something like it, was absolutely mandatory.

ENDLESS OCTOBER

Wool and Gore-Tex, about seven layers deep, constituted the upper body wear.

The only weak point in my system is my gloves. I wear Orvis deerskin hunting gloves. I don't like thicker gloves because they don't have the touch. I was right on the edge of being too cold in the fingers. (In fact, I might need to change my gloves. The search continues for the ultimate cold-weather hunting glove. My kids gave me some new gloves for Christmas this year, and they seem to have what I need. They are Gortex lined and designed for wet and cold.)

As far as the dogs are concerned, the weather really did not bother them at all. Even Ruby, my female Brittany, who is the skinniest of them all and went through the ice into the ankle-deep creek, came out of the bottom and hunted like a champ. I watched her closely, however, and she was doing fine. Another problem you might encounter is keeping the dog water thawed out. I took care of that by putting the container inside the truck. If you're gone long enough it will freeze. But even at 8°, we had no problem.

I would not want to hunt in this weather daily. But the occasional storm provides a lot of opportunity. We found roosters clustered together in shelterbelts and in the cattails.

It was windy and cold and I wasn't real excited as we approached the tree line. Over the years, I've walked this tree line probably 30 times or more. It is situated perfectly with corn on one side and CRP on the other. There are big, tall trees seen for miles in the wheat and cut corn in North Dakota. A friend owns the farm, now retired, and he told me, "Randy, there are lots of birds here. Come on over!"

I learned later, there were people hunting there the day before. "Oh, great!" I thought, "They moved all the birds out of there. This will be just another four-mile walk with the dogs."

The wind was strong from the north, right down the center of the tree line, which was composed of huge old cottonwoods and evergreens, maybe four rows of them.

We put Ace, my main dog, out with Ruby with the intentions of easing over to the end of the row and working straight up it. This wasn't Ace's first time here though. Once the "first put out rodeo" was over, I noticed Ace was no longer with us. I checked my new GPS tracker and saw he was pointed ... in the treeline.

We moved to him, entered the shade of the trees, and saw him locked up. The rooster broke up and out before we could get too close, but Bobby's 20 ga. with Prairie Storm 3" #5's put him dead in the air, just as he cleared the alder row on the edge of the trees. He was a big old beauty.

Ruby locked up, Ace backed (dutifully, but grudgingly) and three roosters took off. I killed a tree and Bobby, again, dropped a bird for the retrieve.

ENDLESS OCTOBER

We worked our way, slowly, to the end of the treeline, with birds coming out the sides, too far ahead to shoot. The dogs were not perfectly disciplined, but close enough I was pleased. Heck, there were so many roosters running around, I wasn't all that disciplined, either!

At the end of the row, Ace locked down and Ruby backed. The bird flushed out away from me, right into Bobby's gun. I think he was a little surprised, but he let it get out a suitable distance and dropped it out in the cut corn. Ace put it in my hand with a tip of the hat to the shooter – praise not easily earned from the experienced gun dog.

After lunch, we put Cap, my 2-year-old by Ace, down and Ruby, again. We worked some smaller tree windbreaks with corn in between. Very little cover and I was not hopeful.

Right out of the box, both dogs got birdy and slowed down, hunkered down and cat-creeped to some blown brush at the edge of the cut corn. For a hundred yards, we pointed, released, pointed, released backing, etc.

One after another, the pups took turns pointing and backing. Finally, after a hundred yards of this, four roosters and two hens blew out of the brush headed for freedom. I was the only one near and it was clear shooting in a target-rich environment, and not one bird went down!

The sun got in my eyes, my alarm clock didn't go off, and a dog ate my homework! I need more excuses! I just missed. Period.

Both dogs looked at me. It was bad.

Cap picked up more scent and worked some CRP. Finally, he pointed hard, and I kicked a big rooster out from a brush pile and put him in the bag.

Another treeline bird bit the dust, further up, after Ruby's fine work; and we headed for the truck, one bird short.

I looked to my left, as we walked and talked; Ruby was locked down in the grass along the trees! As I approached her, a rooster jumped up, tried to fly, couldn't get airborne, and ran!

Ruby went after it, Cap joined the chase, I yelled, "Dead bird, fetch it up!" and the merry chase was on.

At one point, Ruby got a mouthful of feathers, but the bird got away. We worked up and down the trees; until Cap locked up and I walked over, saw the bird hunkered down. I picked it up and dispatched it. I don't know why it didn't fly, I imagine it might have been a bird wounded by the previous hunter, but it still put up a good fight.

I still get excited thinking about that day. Good companionship, good dogs, smart roosters. Sweet.

**Ruby admiring her hero, Cap
(Photo by Randy Schultz in North Dakota)**

RANDY SCHULTZ

**Ruby, Randy, and Cap in North Dakota
(Photo by Bobby Ferris)**

15. North Dakota

As a quail hunter, with quail dogs, the thought of shooting something as big as a rooster pheasant seemed unsportsmanlike. How could you miss a big white, red, and green bird? Well, it happened to a friend.

I loaded up the diesel and, two days later, showed up in North Dakota with a couple of good dogs, Ruby (S/F), and Rocket (Brit/M), ready to have a go at those big birds. We set up in the southwest corner of the state, because we read they had a good bird population and lots of public land. We purchased licenses and maps and had a talk with the Game Warden about where we could likely find some pheasant.

After a little driving, we dropped the tailgate on a public hunting area near a waterfowl lake. Not really having a plan, I figured a rooster, like most birds, would be hunkered down in thick cover in the draws. So Ruby and Rocket and I started down a draw that had a bunch of cut wheat stretching out on either side. (One thing about those North Dakota wheat fields: They go as far as the eye can see and don't stop for much, unless it can't be plowed.)

The draw had a little creek at the bottom, and I tried to figure out what likely pheasant cover looked like. Suddenly, Rocket locked up tight on a shrub on the edge of the creek. I know my dog, and when old Bonehead corkscrews himself into the ground and gets that glazed look in his eyes, you might as well shoulder the gun and get ready for the flush.

I eased up to the bush, ready for about anything. I kicked and looked and kicked some more and nothing came out. Glancing back at Rocket, he was looking at me and he was starting to loosen up, so I tapped him on the head to release him.

He hit that shrub and snorted around a bunch and then took off on a straight line with his head down to the ground. He went out about 100 yards and spun around again – tighter than a tick on a fat pointer.

One more time, I went in. Once again, nothing. He snorted again and took off.

This time he broke left, went about 150 yards, took a hard right and headed back in to me. 50 yards out, he pointed a clump of grass no bigger than a small cactus.

ENDLESS OCTOBER

I casually walked up with my Fox double over my shoulder ready for more of the same. Just as I reached him, I noticed Ruby had joined the rodeo and was backing on Rocket's other side. "Good," I thought, "we'll head on back to the truck and re-think this evolution as soon as I kick this clump."

As I took one step in front of the dog, the biggest bird I'd ever seen came off the ground, squawking and gaining altitude. I'd like to say I dropped him with one shot, but, truth be told, it took me a bit to get my gun off my shoulder and my head screwed on straight.

I did notice he was beautiful, with red eyes, green head, white neck band, and laughing his head off because he caught me flat-footed with my pants down.

I watched as both dogs chased him out of sight over the wheat fields. They came back a few minutes later and we forgot about lunch and got serious about hunting.

Ruby hit real hard on a little shrub. She was taut, white tail high. This time I went in ready to shoot. When the old rooster came up, he wasn't more than 15 yards away and a load of 20 ga. steel 4's hit him broadside.

Ruby was on him when he hit the ground and she looked up at me like I was pulling a trick on her. "Boss, this ain't a bird, it's a horse!"

She managed to pick it up and deliver it to hand for a fine retrieve. (That bird is in my den, tail and head high.)

We had a great week working those North Dakota birds. For a guy who thought it would be easy, we found out just how hard it can be. We did learn how easy it is to tell the difference between hens and roosters. (Unless, of course, they take off right in to the sun. Even though they were squawking, we let a few of them go, because we couldn't see the colors.)

Rocket learned about retrieving wounded birds and all about those spurs on the feisty old roosters; and we learned about the skunk population.

With a 3 bird limit, we wanted to spread the hunting out over the day, so we concentrated on the quality rather than the quantity. I only shot pointed birds, not birds bumped by the dogs or kicked up by me. Still, there was plenty of action, and the dogs (and my legs) got a lot of work.

Most years, this part of North Dakota has a lot of birds; probably due to the wheat and CRP. The people are very nice, and they'll even pull your truck out of a ditch, if you need it.

Most of the land around here is posted, so you need permission to hunt; and a lot of the land is leased, available for a fee.

But there is plenty of public land (Private Land Open to Sportsmen, PLOTS), so the opportunities are plentiful. In North

Dakota (when this was written), non-posted land can be hunted without permission, but we always ask anyway, as a courtesy to the landowner.

If you are in that part of North Dakota in late October, look for the blue F-250, Jones trailer, and boneheaded Brittany. We'll swap some lies and chase some wily Ringnecks. We might even miss a few.

Happy Ruby and Blue Quail

16. Thinking Texas Blues

"The darn things run, don't fly, and will mess up a dog."

That's what I'd heard about Blues, or Scaled Quail, from just about everyone I know who'd hunted them. So I packed up the Jones trailer with a load of good quail dogs, grabbed my Fox double from under the bed and headed out to Texas.

I know most folks don't think of Blue Quail when they think of Texas, but out in the western edge of the Panhandle, hard up against New Mexico, there's a bunch of parched, pokey land that holds nothing but Blue Quail, or scalies, as the local hunters call them.

When we arrived, they hadn't seen rain in five months and the ranchers were worried most about fire. The place we hunted was a cattle ranch with (wind) mills and tanks on every pasture, so there was plenty of water for the birds and the cows. Pasture is the technical term, but there were eight 4,000 acre enclosures of sand, grass, cactus, and scrub. A Southern bird dog man like me likes to hunt objectives-tree lines, field edges, draws, and gullies.

You could start in any direction here and not hit anything worth going around as far as you could walk in hours. It was stark. But it did hold the birds.

The owner took me around the place, showing me tanks and the general lay of the land (including some 1,000+ year old Indian glyphs, like you see on television, down in holes carved in solid rock by running water.) and that took about four hours. Then we exchanged cell numbers in case the truck got stuck and we were on our own.

We parked on the edge of a road that was Texas on one side and New Mexico on the other and I put old Bo (my setter male) on the ground. We headed down what looked like a draw looking for something that flew.

After 20 minutes or so, on the southern exposure of the draw, Bo slammed still and I hurried up to him, Kicking around at the base of a cactus plant and not getting anything up, I noticed Bo was looking over his right shoulder, his tail was coming down and his attention was really not on the job at hand. He was too broke to move, but he was telling me, "Boss, the birds aren't here – they're over there."

ENDLESS OCTOBER

I tapped him on the head and he broke to the right, looped around to the left and locked up at the base of a pile of scrub. Just as I was about to kick the pile, what looked like 20 gray blurs exploded out of the pile going in every point of the compass, I managed to drop one and felt pretty lucky to do that.

I saw it fall, marked it and called Bo over for the retrieve. He couldn't find the little thing. I was giving him some encouragement (telling him I'd get another dog, if he didn't do his job and find that bird), but it took a while and I managed to spot it. It was so dry, and the birds were "air washed" – they had no scent when they hit the ground. (You'd better really mark them down or, good dog or not, you'll lose a bunch of them.)

As we eased out of the draw, we came up on a water tank. It didn't take much coaxing to get the dogs into the cold wet. Water is the key to everything out here. Where you find water and grass, you'll find birds (and sand spurs). After a day or so of hunting these gray ghosts like we hunt the bobwhites back home, hunting edges and objectives, I realized that ALL of the birds we found were within a half-mile of a water tank.

Well, the story just got interesting! We'd drive close to a tank and start a loop all the way around it (far out to close in) and, every time, we'd hit one or two large coveys. This was a blast.

Interestingly, although their reputation is one of flightiness and running away, there were numerous times we did everything but dig the bush up and throw it in the air to get the birds to flush.

Also, many times they'd flush toward a stand of low cactus and knee-high grass and disappear. When we got there, we'd cover the area and maybe get a find or two, figuring the rest of the 30 bird covey ran out of there. Then, once, Bo locked up tight looking up into a cactus! He's experienced and I can rely on him, so I eased on up, ready to shoot, looking on the ground around the Cholla cactus. Right about eye level, 8-10 birds blasted off as I got close to the bush. They were IN the cactus!

From then on, those cacti were dubbed "quail trees" and we broke the code on those scamps. It was amazing the number of times those birds would never hit the ground after a flush. There was no wonder the dogs had a hard time picking up the scent!

I've been back there a few times and, landowner willing, I'll go back again. The allure of this place isn't so much the quantity of birds as it is the land itself. Dry, gritty, windy, sharp and unforgiv-ing, yet it is a beautiful place, too. People lived here thousands of years ago (I know because I read their mail in that water-carved hole) and lived a good life. I can see how this place could gnaw on you and bring you back year after year, thinking about those Texas blues.

ENDLESS OCTOBER

**Arizona rainbow and hunter Robert Siler
(Photo by Randy Schultz)**

17. Arizona Quail

When a buddy, who lives in Mesa, Arizona, told me about the good quail hunting near his home, I politely questioned his sanity. Hunt quail in Arizona? The place is full of sun, sand, cactus, and Yankees (no offense to my Northern friends), but quail? In fact, there is a tremendous opportunity for the quail hunter in Arizona. Within an hour's drive of the Phoenix airport, you can be in some serious quail country.

I decided to fly and take Bo, my setter. He's my senior dog, experienced on pheasant, grouse, Huns, Chukar, quail and woodcock. I figured he'd do the best at helping me corral a few of the local birds.

We flew into Phoenix and drove to Globe, Arizona (about an hour east), bought a license and asked around about where to hunt.

"How you doing? You do any bird hunting around here?"

would usually get the conversation started in the direction I wanted to go.

While I was under no illusions as to finding secret "honey holes," the local boys were really helpful and directed us to the area north of Roosevelt Lake, in the midst of the Tonto National Forest (a gazillion acres of public land. The name is a misnomer, because where we were there wasn't a tree in sight, just cactus and sand.)

We found out early where the birds were: around any water available. That might be stock tanks, creeks, or just mud holes.

The maps of the area designate Forest Service roads, so we drove up a likely one and put the dogs on the ground. After maybe 15 minutes, Bo locked up near a catch pen and stock tank (full of water from a windmill).

Not really knowing what to expect, I eased on up to the tank and saw about 50 birds running though the bushes up the side of the hill! Those little guys can scoot.

I kicked around a little, but Bo had seen enough and he headed out after the covey. About 50 yards out, he locked up on a big prickly pear cactus surrounded by a bunch of scrub.

I ran over to him and kicked all over that brush pile. I could have raised the dead with the commotion, but nothing came out. I thought we'd just missed them, so I reached down to tap Bo on the head and release him. Whoosh! Three birds blew out of that pile — going different directions.

I looked like a bobcat jumping a covey; head looking everywhere at once and totally confused. I managed to spray some shot around, but those birds were seriously gone by the time I pulled trigger.

Not only could they run, but when they decided to take to the air, they really blasted off! Bo gave me the evil eye, "Nice shooting, boss!"

We kept working up the little draw. With mountains on both sides, Bo hit scent again and froze. This time, I was ready for the little bombers, and when four of them came out from under a bush I managed to drop one.

Bo made a good retrieve and we sat down to admire the bird. He was a male Gambels Quail — brightly colored with a little topknot. He was beautiful.

I slid him into the bird bag and we moved on. We worked up one side of the little valley and managed to get points and shots all along the side of the hill.

It was a good year for quail: they had plenty of rain that spring, and we were running into separate coveys. My partner moved on down to the bottom of the valley, and I heard him shoot on three separate occasions in a one-hour period.

ENDLESS OCTOBER

When we met for a sit and a sandwich at the head of the canyon, I asked him about his luck. His eyes were still as big as saucers over a covey he swears was 100 birds that got up right under his dog and scared the devil out of both of them.

The coveys were big and shooting was constant. It was a great time watching Bo work those birds under a sky so blue it is impossible to describe, with sharp craggy peaks on either side of us.

Not all was roses and honey, though. Bo and I found out all about Cholla cactus. Cholla cacti look like link sausages growing in a small bush. The dog will run by one and a link will break off and hook in to a dog's side and aggravate him until he reaches around to pull it out with his mouth. Then it'll get into his mouth and it's a mess at that point. The spines are barbed and they are difficult to get out – eventually they'll get infected.

The best method I found to avoid the problem is to hunt at higher elevations where the Cholla isn't. Local dogs see and avoid the Cholla, but old Bo had to learn the hard way. (There's a good vet in Globe if old Biscuit really gets tied up.)

If cactus spines get on your dog's legs or body, we found the best method to get them out is to carry a comb and just brush them off, then picking the remaining spines out by hand. Boots for the dogs are a must, especially if you are going to hunt for more than a few days. Pads get worn down by the volcanic ash and crushed rock. Boots will give your dogs some protection from low-growing cactus. You'd better take some chaps, too. I once shot a covey on the rise just as a prickly pear cactus snapped back on to my leg! Now, that burned! (I missed the bird, too!)

I quickly headed back to the truck for my double-tin chaps. Water is real important! Take bottles for you and the dog; even though there are stock tanks around, you can't bet on it. As a general rule, give it all to the dog.

Gambels, Scaled (Blue), and Mearns quail are all indigenous to Arizona. But Gambels quail are most numerous in this area and plenty of sport to hunt. A buddy of mine made the comment that hunting quail in Arizona is a lot like big game hunting. It's hard work. I know what he means. I was as proud of those birds in my bag at the end of the day as my Moose in Alaska or Whitetail in Georgia! I know I was proud of my old dog Bo, too. I admired at the way he climbed out of the canyons following scent, just to head back down.

In December, the temperature at the higher elevations can be pretty cool (we hit 19 one night) and the days range from the 50s to the 70s. One time, it even rained for 2 days! That made for great hunting and scenting. (But you had to be concerned about the dirt track roads: they got slick, and stream crossings were, at times, problematic.)

Even if Arizona wasn't covered in quail, just walking

through the beauty of the canyons and listening to nothing but the sigh of the breeze would be enough for me to head back. The jagged peaks are so close sometimes; they are hard to focus upon, silhouetted against that intense blue sky. It's a stark, dry, prickly, mesmerizing land, loaded with hard-running, hard-flying little buzz bombs that will challenge you and your dog.

Ace and Sharptail Grouse

18. Montana Big Sky Birds

It's hard to get excited about hunting when the temperature outside is hitting 95 to 100 degrees every day, but for years I'd been pondering early season Sharptail Grouse hunting in Montana. I called a friend up there, and he said the birds were plentiful and the season opened on 1 September – perfect! I packed Bo, Peaches, and Ace into the Jones trailer and off we went to Montana to hunt Sharptail Grouse.

Sharpies love the wide-open spaces in Montana. In fact,

ENDLESS OCTOBER

Montana is pretty much at the southern end of their range, which goes all the way into Alaska. The state started the Block Management Program plan a few years ago, and I was a bit skeptical as to how that would work. It involves ordering a book and map from the state, finding enrolled land, and then calling the office to get the phone number of the rancher. Then, meeting the farmer and getting a permission slip to hunt.

It didn't sound like a good plan to me. But, as usual, I was dead wrong. Not only was there plenty of BMA land available, it was easy to find, and the ranchers were, to a man, very helpful and friendly.

Usually, they'd give you tips on where to find the birds. Also, if you saw a nice piece of land in the program, the farmer's name and phone number are posted on the fence and you could give him a call and bypass the state folks.

Often, the biggest problem we had with the system was getting out of the rancher's house to hunt. These nice folks liked to visit!

This time of year, the birds like to feed in the alfalfa bottoms along the creeks and rivers. Ranchers build dikes around the fields to hold the winter snowmelt, and, in September, the alfalfa has been cut and the re-growth is coming up about ankle to shin high. The birds hunker down in the middle of those fields, coming out occasionally to graze through the adjoining wheat fields.

We did some looking around the first day and settled on some BMP land a little south of us. Water in the creek and huge alfalfa fields settled the deal.

After signing in, I opened the dog trailer door and let old Bo stretch his legs a little. There was a lot of bouncing around, and dogs whining, and trying to find the right shells, hat, and whistle going on, but, after a few minutes, we headed up the draw towards some alfalfa fields surrounded by cut wheat.

This is wide-open country, not unlike Texas, so a quail-trained dog can do well here. Bo was in his element! Eight years old, experienced and fit, he took off up one side of the draw for a bit and down the other side. The rolling terrain and hills made watching his white, snapping tail a breeze.

He headed up the side of a steep hill, working all the low scrub bushes along the way, while I tried to figure out where I'd be if I was a Sharpie.

After a minute of wondering what the working folks were doing this fine September day, I noticed I wasn't hearing his bell. Sure enough he was locked up on a patch of low shrubs about half way up the side of a steep hill!

Early in the year, this could be almost anything, but he was swearing to it, eating scent and tighter than a fat tick on a pointer. As I eased up to him, about 20 reddish-brown buzz bombs exploded out of the brush pile and headed out up the hill – Hungarian Partridge.

I dropped one and threw lead at another and, suddenly, a good day in the field became a great day!

After the retrieve, we sat down for a minute to admire the bird, then bagged him up and headed into the alfalfa. It was already getting hot (about 70 degrees) so I watered the campaigner and took it easy on my legs – walking easily along the coulee. (As with most land in the plains, water is a huge factor. Take plenty with you, enough for you and your dog – and give it all to the dog.)

Bo hit the alfalfa field in stride, working into the wind and birdy from the minute his feet touched the green. He slammed still right in the middle of the patch as I hurried up to him, aiming for a point about 20 yards upwind of his nose. That dog's tail started to drop and his head came up a little and he begged to be released, and, sure enough, I kicked around and got nothing.

I tapped him on the head to release him, and he immediately went in his "They're right here, boss, give me a minute to lock 'em down!" mode.

Tail low, head to the ground, weaving back and forth, methodical and intense, he worked his way 40 yards up the field before slamming to a point – tail high, head high, and still as a statue!

By this time, I was as excited as Bo, checking to make sure

I had the old 20 ga. Fox loaded with #6's, and hustled along behind him.

The colors are brighter and the sounds more intense when that old bird dog tells me we have birds "right here!"

About 20 steps in front of him, 10 big gray Sharpies got up and headed out. It sounded like they were laughing as they made their patented "nuh, nuh, nuh" sound when they flew.

I managed to knock one down and watched the rest fly to the other end of the field and settle down again. Bo brought me the dead bird and we looked at it for a bit, got some water, and headed on down the field to find some more.

Early in the season, the birds haven't been shot at and they don't fly far – if you watch them after the flush, you'll probably see them land. Since they don't run like a pheasant, you might be able to pick them up again.

We worked our way from field to field, usually finding birds in or around the edges of each one. This area was loaded with Sharptail Grouse.

Not only Sharpies and Huns (Hungarian Partridge) enjoy the hospitality of the alfalfa and hillsides, but also Sage Grouse. Neither Bo nor I had ever seen one of those monsters. On one of his long casts, he locked up at the end of a field about 100 yards away and, as I got to him, I swear he had a different look on his face. I took a few steps upwind and you'd think they'd scrambled all the bombers out of Ellsworth Air Force Base! Six big, hulking, huge birds rumbled down the field and lifted into the air heading for parts unknown. It rocked me back a little to see the size of those bad boys! In fact, I didn't know what they were (so I didn't shoot), but I knew they weren't Sharpies or Huns.

After an instant replay and a lot of pondering and discussion we came to the realization they were Sage Grouse- magnificent birds!

We hunted until noon every day until the heat drove us back to the motel for a siesta. About 5 p.m., we headed out again to a different farm for more hunting.

The temps started out in the 50s each morning and hit the high 80s in the afternoons before cooling off, with the low humidity, as the sun headed for the horizon. It was a good excuse to rest the dogs (and my legs) this early in the season.

We swapped out dogs, too, every chance we had, and made real sure they had water and shade for rest.

About the fourth day, as the only bird hunters in the area, we drew the attention of the game warden from Glendive. He was pleasant, professional, and very thorough – and a fount of knowledge as we pumped him with questions about the area and the birds.

These guys are a great source of information and I recommend asking them everything you can think of while they are there. They are spread pretty thin (kind of like Texas Rangers, I think), so use 'em while you got 'em.

Between the heat and the drive and the dusty roads, we realized we were having a great time. The birds were plentiful, the land is available, and the folks are friendly. This is a great way to get an early season hunt, tune up old Biscuit and use that rarely bestowed kitchen pass all at once. Give the early season Sharptails in Montana a look. We were glad we did. It's an annual trip, one we're happy to take every year.

Ruby and Sharptail Grouse

19. A Good Day

As I was driving off the ranch in Texas after a frustrating day, I was thinking about moving on up to South Dakota, when I saw a bird flush to my left. I quickly stopped, grabbed my gun, my dog Ace, and a pocket of shells, and I stepped off the graded sand road of the ranch.

I took one step and the world exploded at my feet when 30 blues got up all around me. I mean, I stepped into the middle of them, and a bunch more ran off into the brush. Ace locked up to the flush and I watched as they scattered out along a stretch of flat, brushy, sandy, grazed-over pasture.

The sun was at my back, the breeze was in my face, it was 30 degrees and there was a smile on my face as I set out to some great shooting.

Ace locked up time after time pointing two or three of the little buzz bombs before they erupted out of the cactus, shin-oak, or grass pile. We took our time, easing along and hitting all the cover, ditches and vegetation.

What seemed like five minutes later (actually an hour or so), I grabbed for more shells and came up empty – with a dog on point, the sun on the horizon and the temperature dropping fast.

I had one shell left in the A.H.Fox 20 ga. double and was one bird shy of the limit here in Texas.

Limits never held much fascination for me. I rarely get close enough to worry about them on quail, but today it would be nice to round it out.

Ace was locked down at the base of a Cholla cactus as I eased on up alongside him. I glanced at his face and it was set in that stony look bird dogs get when they are dead center of the scent cone, mesmerized by the smell.

I kicked at the shrub and five gray blurs came out of that

cactus heading in all points of the compass! As a lefty, I locked down on the one heading from my left to right. I checked his location down the barrels and pulled the trigger. The bird dropped, and Ace was on him for the retrieve.

Suddenly, the nine hours I had spent, working every bit of good cover I could find, didn't seem so bad. Booting and un-booting the dogs, watering them, walking in the sandy bottoms loaded with sand burrs, up the hills and through the draws, picking cactus out the dogs, and myself, wasn't the chore it had seemed only an hour ago.

The whole day was condensed into the last hour.

It was a good day.

Bull Moose in Alaska
(Photo by BJ Schultz)

20. Mama Moose

When I was 16, a friend and I were squirrel hunting outside Anchorage, not far from what is now Alyeska. Our plan was to walk through the fir trees with .22 pistols and watch and listen for squirrels. It wasn't a great plan, but it was better than no plan.

We were separated by a hundred yards, or so, and were acting all grown-up and manly as we hunted. I rounded a big fir tree and saw a cow moose lying down, facing away from me. I knew enough to know I had no business being there, and I was sure the girl was calving. And, I knew that a cow moose will kill a grizzly that comes near her new-born calf!

I didn't stop, blink, or hesitate more than a millisecond. I turned and ran as fast as a healthy, thoroughly scared 16-year-old young man could move.

I had hell on my heels, and I could hear her coming behind me. Her feet were pounding, and she ran right through saplings, grunting, and breathing hard. My only chance at safety was a dead-fall 50 yards ahead of me.

Expecting to feel a hoof in my back at any second, when I got in range, I literally jumped through the air, over a huge downed fir tree log and under a pile of alder brush someone had piled up.

I kept pushing further down into the pile until I was on my back, under the fir tree log, wedged in the eight-inch space between the log and the ground.

I was hugging that tree like it was my girlfriend! My face was turned to the brush pile where I came in, cheek pressed to the rough bark. My pistol was in my right hand, and it was as quiet as I ever heard it in the woods.

It was eerily silent – except for a heavy breathing sound six inches from my face.

I slowly turned my head to the left, and looked right into

the big eye of a seriously pissed-off cow moose, with her ears laid back, and her front lip exposing some big teeth.

She pawed the ground trying to get me, but the logs and sticks protected me. That's when I heard my buddy, Vince, laughing. He was safely up a tree a few yards away, and thought this was all terribly funny.

To this day, I think he waited to start laughing until he knew I wasn't dead, but I'm not real sure on that point.

But here I was, on my back, wedged under a downed fir tree with mama moose trying to kill me.

Five hours later (actually, maybe 10 minutes) she was still there. Just as mad. Finally, I managed to transfer my pistol from my right to left hand, by feel, over my head, without dropping it. Then, I put that muzzle just in front of her nose and fired. The bullet wouldn't hit her (although, I was kind of hoping for a lucky shot to hit my buddy, Vince, the jerk, still laughing his head off.), but she'd feel the blast.

She did jerk back, and it took all six shots from that Ruger revolver, but she finally gave me the stink-eye, one more time, and headed back where I found her.

I gave her quite a while to settle down, and I slid out the back of that brush pile. We shrugged the incident off, and moved to another area to continue our hunt.

ENDLESS OCTOBER

I am more scared now, in the re-telling, than I ever was then. Growing up in Alaska was heaven-on-earth for a kid. We learned a lot about hunting, fishing, and sports outside. Cuts, bruises, broken bones, getting lost and getting found again were part of every summer day. There were few rules, but we'd better not be late for dinner.

Randy and, left to right, Ruby, Cap, Ace
(Photo by Bobby Ferris)

Glossary

Birdy – a term used to mean that a bird dog, by his body action, is signaling that he is smelling bird scent. Being "birdy" is usually followed by the "point."

Brittany – a medium sized pointing dog with short tail and gentle disposition.

Cap- a long ridge or flat-topped hill with steep sides

Chukar – upland game bird found in the high, rocky cliffs of the western United States. Introduced from Asia.

CRP – Conservation Resource Program. Untilled land critically important for game habitat, usually pheasant.

Dakotas – North and/or South Dakota.

Goat Rope – chaos.

GPS – Global Positioning System. An electronic system used to find your exact location.

Hungarian Partridge (Hun)- upland gamebird, slightly larger than a quail, that lives in the Great Plains. Introduced from Europe.

Location – a Pad of gravel upon which to build a pump jack.

NSTRA – National Shoot to Retrieve Field Trial Association.

Oil patch – a large geographical area over a large oil field.

Public Land – land owned by the United State Federal Government or the States.

Pump Jack – the machine that actually pumps oil out of the ground in an up and down motion.

Pheasant – a large, colorful, upland game bird usually near corn, wheat, and CRP. Introduced from China.

Ruffed Grouse – an upland gamebird that lives in the northern forests.

ENDLESS OCTOBER

Sharptail Grouse – an upland game bird that lives in the grasses of the Prairie.
Shot Shells – containers that hold gunpowder and round lead shot, to be used in shotguns. Similar in use to bullets.
Tracking Collars – electronic device worn by a dog to show the owner the dog's location.
Valley Quail – an upland game bird in the northwest United States.

About the Author

Randy grew up in Anchorage, Alaska. From his father, he learned to appreciate the outdoors and an athletic lifestyle. After college, at Oregon State University, he followed his father's and two brother's footsteps into the Navy, became a Naval Aviator, and flew off numerous aircraft carriers. In 1979, he left the Navy to fly airliners for Delta Airlines. Along with flying for Delta, he continued flying in the Naval Reserves, retiring in 1993. After 27 years, in 2005, he also retired from Delta Airlines. Since then, Randy has been pursuing his passion of raising, training, and hunting his Brittany bird dogs. He enjoys traveling around the country, from September to February, hunting several different species of upland gamebirds. Randy published articles in several magazines. He blogs about his adventures, and reviews hunting-related products, at

www.abirdhuntersthoughts.com.

His Podcast, "A Bird Hunter's Thoughts – Turn 'Em Loose" is available on Apple and all major platforms. He lives in Zebulon, Georgia, with his wife, five bird dogs, a Groodle, and one fat Lab.

Contact: rbjfarm@gmail.com

ENDLESS OCTOBER

Pearlie
(Photo by Randy Schultz)

Made in the USA
Monee, IL
23 October 2020